Druidism

How Ancient Druid Practices Can Enrich Your Life Today

(Exploring the Mysteries of Celtic Wisdom and Magic)

Stephen Montoya

Published By **Elena Holly**

Stephen Montoya

Druidism: How Ancient Druid Practices Can Enrich Your Life Today (Exploring the Mysteries of Celtic Wisdom and Magic)

ISBN 978-1-9995143-9-6

No part of this guidebook shall be reproduced in any form without permission in writing from the publisher except in the case of brief quotations embodied in critical articles or reviews.

Legal & Disclaimer

The information contained in this book is not designed to replace or take the place of any form of medicine or professional medical advice. The information in this book has been provided for educational & entertainment purposes only.

The information contained in this book has been compiled from sources deemed reliable, and it is accurate to the best of the Author's knowledge; however, the Author cannot guarantee its accuracy and validity and cannot be held liable for any errors or omissions. Changes are periodically made to this book. You must consult your doctor or get professional medical advice before using any of the suggested remedies, techniques, or information in this book.

Table Of Contents

Chapter 1: Origins And Evolution

The journey of statistics Druidry consists of delving into its Celtic roots and the subsequent metamorphoses that have usual this ancient way of life into what it is nowadays. In this financial ruin, we're capable of discover the origins of Druidic practices, their historic evolution, and the impact of external cultures and historic events on their development.

The Celtic Roots

Druidry exhibits its origins a number of the Celtic human beings, a various organization of Iron Age tribes spread throughout Western Europe, collectively with factors of modern-day-day Ireland, Scotland, Wales, England, France, and Germany. The Druids have been the located beauty internal the ones societies, serving a mess of roles beginning from non secular leaders and judges to college students and advisors to the tribal chiefs.

Unlike other non secular traditions that could rely on a number one text or a unique narrative, Druidry changed into in big element oral in nature. The teachings were passed down through generations within the form of myths, memories, songs, and rituals. The Druids themselves underwent rigorous schooling, frequently lasting up to 20 years, to memorize tremendous quantities of information. They had been reliable as the holders of cultural records, which covered not in reality religious beliefs but moreover understanding of regulation, technological expertise, and the arts.

Roman Influence and Christianization

The arrival of the Romans in the British Isles at a few stage inside the number one century BCE had a profound impact on the local Celtic tribes and, by using the usage of extension, on Druidry. The Romans noticed the Druids as a big political and religious strain that needed to be both incorporated or extinguished. Roman writers like Julius Caesar left payments detailing Druidic practices, despite the fact that the ones had been frequently colored by using the political and imperial dreams of the authors.

The next Christianization of the British Isles similarly diluted Druidic have an impact on. Many Druidic traditions had been subsumed beneath Christian practices that allows you to convert the community population. For instance, holy net web sites like wells and groves were regularly rededicated to Christian saints, and plenty of Druidic recollections and deities had been included into the Christian narrative. During the medieval period, Druids have been often depicted in literature as wizards or soothsayers, similarly divorcing their image from the respected discovered beauty they as soon as have been.

The Druidic Revival and Modern Adaptations

In the seventeenth and 18th centuries, hobby in Druidry resurfaced as part of the broader Romantic motion. The Druidic Revival, as it is recognized, have become characterized with the aid of a renewed interest in historical languages, folklore, and non secular practices. However, loads of the revival turn out to be based totally on resourceful reconstructions as opposed to rigorous ancient evidence, frequently mixing Druidic symbolism with then-famous esoteric thoughts.

The twentieth and twenty first centuries have visible in addition evolutions of Druidic practices, inspired by way of way of ecological moves and the New Age. Modern Druidry is greater eclectic and attracts from some of assets, which encompass reconstructed Celtic rituals, Eastern philosophies, or even Wiccan factors. Contemporary Druids are frequently worried in ecological activism, emphasizing the interconnectedness of all lifestyles and the sanctity of nature, values that harken lower lower back to the Druidic reverence for the herbal international.

Druidic Philosophy

The Interconnectedness of All Things

One of the foundational tenets of Druidic philosophy is the interconnectedness of all subjects. This is not just a spiritual concept but furthermore an ecological one, because it displays an knowledge of the way all existence workplace paintings are a part of a larger surroundings. From the macroscopic to the microscopic, the whole thing is connected in a complex net of relationships. The Druidic view aligns properly with contemporary ecological theories which emphasize systems questioning, acknowledging that each problem of an ecosystem has an essential feature to play.

Druids traditionally espouse the view that people are part of nature, now not other than it. This outlook encourages respectful interplay with all elements of the natural international, which includes animals, flora, or maybe inanimate gadgets like rocks and rivers. One can discover echoes of this thoughts-set in cutting-edge environmentalism, which calls for a sustainable dating with nature. In a international grappling with the effects of climate alternate, habitat loss, and biodiversity decline, adopting a Druidic mind-set of interconnectedness can foster a experience of duty and urgency to take full-size motion.

Reverence for Nature

Another critical thing of Druidic philosophy is a deep reverence for nature. This is possibly what Druidry is most famous for. In Druidic traditions, nature isn't an insignificant backdrop for human activity however a living entity deserving of recognize and care. Sacred groves, stone circles, and herbal springs are often focal points for Druidic rituals, emphasizing the importance of herbal settings. The Earth is regularly taken into consideration a goddess determine, a divine manifestation that sustains all existence.

The reverence for nature extends to individual factors as well, every attributed with unique properties and developments that contribute to the whole. For instance, every type of tree, animal, or maybe celestial body just like the moon and stars have specific symbolic meanings in Druidic lore. These factors are not simplest vital for their practical uses but are also imbued with religious significance. In modern-day phrases, this perspective can promote a more sustainable manner of residing, as one learns to charge herbal belongings, now not only for their application, however for his or her inherent genuinely really well worth.

The Quest for Wisdom and Inspiration

The very last middle guiding precept of Druidic philosophy to be cited proper right here is the non-prevent quest for statistics and notion. Unlike some religious paths that emphasize the attainment of a selected state of enlightenment as an last motive, Druidry sees knowledge as a adventure in choice to a holiday spot. Learning is lifelong, and knowledge comes from direct enjoy, introspection, and interaction with each the herbal and supernatural worlds.

"Awen" is a important concept on this regard, regularly defined because of the reality the glide of spirit, perception, or divine illumination. While it is going to be explored in extra element in a later financial disaster, it suffices to say here that Awen is what Druids are searching out in their practices—be it via meditation, ritual, or direct interaction with nature. The regular look for Awen makes Druidry a dynamic and ever-evolving course, it really is especially relevant in a cutting-edge-day-day global that is usually in flux.

Understanding the Druidic Concept of Inspiration

The Symbolism of Awen

The term Awen is regularly represented symbolically as three rays descending from 3 dots. Each ray and dot includes unique meanings. The rays generally represent earth, sea, and sky, which additionally may be understood as body, thoughts, and spirit, on the equal time because the 3 dots represent the triple additives of divinity: maiden, mother, and crone or the god, goddess, and the all-encompassing spirit. In some interpretations, the 3 rays also are visible as facts, expertise, and love.

The photograph of Awen is implemented in plenty of contexts within Druidic practices. It is a part of rituals, engraved into ritual system, or maybe used in tattoos or exceptional sorts of private expression.

When drawn or invoked, it serves to channel the established energy of idea into the cloth realm. The photograph is often voiced via a chant or song, further activating its sturdy energies.

The Role of Awen in Spiritual Practices

Awen performs a substantial feature in non secular practices, each in solitary rituals and communal gatherings. During rites and ceremonies, invoking Awen is concept to carry down the divine essence into the earthly plane. It is often invoked on the start of rituals, to beneficial useful resource in setting intentions, and at the quit, to seal the work that has been completed. Awen additionally serves as a conduit for messages from the opportunity nation-states, facilitating divination and mediumship.

Chapter 2: Sacred Sites

Exploring the Importance of Natural Landscapes Like Stonehenge and Forest Groves in Druidry

Druidry places great emphasis on the sanctity and importance of herbal landscapes, thinking about them to be gateways to religious enlightenment. These sacred internet websites—starting from megalithic stone circles to secluded woodland groves—are crucial to the Druidic enjoy and practices. In this financial disaster, we delve into the importance of such locations, exploring the location they have achieved historically and the significance they hold for modern-day practitioners of Druidry.

Megalithic Sites: Stonehenge and Beyond

One of the most famend megalithic websites associated with Druidry is Stonehenge. Located in Wiltshire, England, this prehistoric monument includes massive status stones organized in concentric circles. Although the original builders and the suitable motive of Stonehenge are topics of continuing debate amongst archaeologists, it's miles extensively believed to were a middle of spiritual, astronomical, and probable even restoration activities. While present day Druids have been no longer the creators of Stonehenge, they have got adopted it as a symbolic center for gatherings, specifically at some point of solstices and equinoxes. It serves as a region in which the Druid community can come together to carry out rituals, meditations, and feature fun their connection with the Earth and the universe.

However, Stonehenge is however one of many megalithic internet websites scattered in the course of the British Isles and Europe. Other huge places embody Avebury, additionally in England, and the Callanish Stones in Scotland. Megalithic web sites regularly characteristic potent energetic focal elements. The stones are believed to channel the Earth's energies, thereby amplifying the spiritual impact of Druidic rituals and practices completed there. Whether it's miles the alignment of the stones with celestial our our bodies or the geomagnetic houses of the floor on which they stand, those websites are considered to be conduits for religious exploration and enlightenment.

Forest Groves: The Green Temples

Equally sacred however a lot much less large are the herbal wooded place groves. Unlike megalithic web web sites, those do now not require complex systems; the timber themselves are considered pillars that hold religious importance. Druids often locate groves to be exceptional locations for solitary rituals, meditations, and communion with nature. Forests have commonly completed an crucial function in Celtic and Druidic mythology, symbolizing the untamed essence of existence and serving as abodes for numerous deities and spirits. Trees like the oak, yew, and ash are especially reputable, and their presence regularly marks a wooded place as an area of specific spiritual energy.

In a grove, the energies are more subtle in comparison to the raw depth at megalithic net web sites. Many Druids find out those natural temples to be greater to be had and versatile, facilitating a big sort of spiritual practices—from energy paintings to divination. The groves are not genuinely spaces for human sports activities but are considered dwelling entities themselves, deserving admire and care. Consequently, a part of the Druidic practice in those regions consists of acts of upkeep and conservation, aligning with the center Druidic precept of dwelling harmoniously with the Earth.

Modern Urban Sacred Spaces

While historical megalithic websites and secluded groves remain crucial, cutting-edge

Druidry has additionally discovered strategies to adapt the concept of sacred areas to contemporary settings. For town Druids who do not have smooth get entry to to such conventional web web sites, options can variety from small home altars to community gardens. The idea is to create a area that permits a reference to the herbal global and serves as a focal point for spiritual practices. While these areas can also moreover furthermore lack the grandeur of a Stonehenge or the serenity of a secluded grove, the underlying thoughts stay the identical: to honor and connect to the Earth and to function a gateway for non secular exploration.

The Druidic Wheel of the Year

Understanding the Eight Festivals

1. Samhain (suggested 'Sah-ween'): Usually celebrated from October 31st to November 1st, Samhain marks the begin of the Celtic New Year. It's a time for honoring

ancestors and the spirit realm. Being a liminal time even as the veil amongst worlds is thin, it's far taken into consideration an opportune length for divination and verbal exchange with the departed.

2.   Yule/Alban Arthan: Coinciding with the Winter Solstice, Yule celebrates the rebirth of the solar and the promise of spring to come back lower lower back. Occurring spherical December 21st, Yule customs encompass lights fires or candles to symbolize the returning light.

three. Imbolc: Celebrated spherical February 1st or 2d, Imbolc heralds the primary signs and signs of spring and is related to the goddess Brigid. It is a time for purification and new beginnings.

4.   Ostara/Alban   Eilir: Corresponding with the Spring Equinox round March twenty first, Ostara celebrates stability and renewal. It marks a time of increasing sunlight hours and is frequently celebrated

with symbols of fertility collectively with eggs and hares.

five.   Beltane: Falling on May 1st, Beltane celebrates the height of spring and the onset of summer time. Known because the Fire Festival, bonfires are a vital part of the festivities, regularly accompanied with the resource of dances and maypole rituals.

6.   Litha/Alban Hefin: Celebrated round June twenty first, Litha coincides with the Summer Solstice. It is the longest day and the shortest night time of the year, symbolizing the sun at its pinnacle.

7.   Lughnasadh: Occurring round August 1st, Lughnasadh marks the begin of the harvest season. Named after the Celtic god Lugh, it's far a time for games, feasting, and thanksgiving for the Earth's bounties.

8.   Mabon/Alban Elfed: Celebrated spherical September twenty first, Mabon corresponds with the Autumn Equinox. It is a time for reflection, gratitude, and for

honoring the declining power of the solar as wintry weather methods.

The Significance of the Wheel

The Druidic Wheel of the Year serves as a religious roadmap, permitting a deeper information of herbal rhythms and cycles. Each festival acts as a waypoint, a pause for reflected photograph, and an possibility to connect to extraordinary additives of the herbal worldwide. In essence, the Wheel of the Year encourages mindfulness of the seasonal modifications which have an impact on no longer definitely the Earth but furthermore human existence.

The timing of these gala's, synchronized with sun and lunar ranges, underscores the tricky dating Druids preserve with celestial activities. This affinity for the cosmos isn't simply an ode to antiquity but a holistic attitude that can be profoundly grounding within the modern-day age, an generation frequently indifferent from natural timelines.

Incorporating the Wheel into Modern Life

The rich tapestry of rituals, traditions, and emblems related to the Druidic Wheel of the Year offers a wellspring of perception for cutting-edge practitioners. While it cannot be possible to have an excellent time every opposition with complex rituals, simpler practices can however provide a deep enjoy of connection. For instance, lighting a candle at the nighttime of the Winter Solstice or getting equipped a harvest dinner party for the duration of Lughnasadh can be strong approaches to mark these activities.

Moreover, the wheel gives an extremely good framework for placing intentions or dreams, non-public or communal. Each pageant's particular energy and symbolism can feature a manual for unique components of life, from non-public increase to community constructing. Integrating those into your annual cycle can offer a based however bendy approach to self-development.

Samhuinn: Ancestor Worship and the Druid New Year

The Dual Nature of Samhuinn

Samhuinn serves as a religious fulcrum round which numerous dualities rotate. One of the maximum conspicuous dualities is life and loss of life. The opposition marks the time whilst the veil some of the bodily international and the spiritual realm is at its thinnest, making it less complicated to talk with ancestral spirits. The Druids bear in mind that the ancestors can offer know-how and steering, especially as one navigates the tough winter months.

Chapter 3: The Winter Solstice

Understanding the Importance of Celebrating the Darkest Day of the Year

In Druidic lifestyle, the Winter Solstice, called Alban Arthan, is a pivotal factor inside the Wheel of the Year. Occurring round December twentieth to 23rd in the Northern Hemisphere, this competition marks the longest night and the shortest day of the yr. In Druidic workout, it signifies the rebirth of the Sun, symbolizing the endless cycle of loss of lifestyles and rebirth that is inherent in nature. This bankruptcy objectives to offer an in-depth exploration of the traditions, symbolism, and current-day packages of Alban Arthan.

Symbolic Interpretations

The term "Alban Arthan" is normally idea to come lower back lower back from a Welsh term, with "Alban" which means "slight of" and "Arthan" signifying "winter" or likely "Arthur," drawing a symbolic link to the mythical King Arthur, who changed into moreover seen as a solar deity. In a deeply symbolic revel in, the Winter Solstice marks a 2d of rebirth, now not truly of the physical sun, but of the inner slight inside all of us. As the sun begins its new cycle, so can humans take the opportunity to begin anew, casting away antique behavior, thoughts, or relationships that now not serve them.

The Oak King and the Holly King, foundational figures in Celtic and Druidic mythology, are said to do struggle times a 365 days, on the Summer and Winter Solstices. At Alban Arthan, the Oak King defeats the Holly King, signifying the bypass decrease returned of longer days and the waning power of wintry climate. The Holly King may want to have his revenge on the Summer Solstice, however for now, the ascendancy of the Oak King reigns, signaling a time of choice and renewal.

Ritual Practices and Traditions

Traditional rituals eventually of Alban Arthan frequently contain lights fires or candles to represent the cross returned of mild. Some Druids can also hold a vigil at some degree in the longest night time, meditating or reflecting on the beyond 365 days and setting intentions for the year in advance. It is a time for internal art work, for understanding one's deeper wishes and goals and laying plans to attain them. Others can also carry out rituals to honor sun deities or the spirits of the land, to are looking for their benefits for the fertile seasons to return.

A commonplace workout is the Yule log rite. A log of o.K.Is regularly added into the house and adorned with greenery and emblems. Some households carve runes or symbols into the wooden, representing their hopes and plans for the imminent seasons. The log is then burned in a fire, and its ashes are often amassed to use in spells or as fertilizers for the coming planting season, thereby linking the event to future cycles of growth and rot.

Trees keep a particular importance in Druidry, and ultimately of Alban Arthan, evergreens like pine, spruce, and fir are given unique hobby. These timber, which stay green even within the darkest days of wintry weather, represent the long-lasting nature of life even within the face of adversity. Decorating evergreen trees or bringing evergreen boughs into the house is a manner of honoring the resilience of lifestyles and the promise of the seasons to return returned.

Modern-Day Applications

Today, the Winter Solstice is often overshadowed with the useful resource of the use of distinct cultural and religious holidays, however its essence can however provide significant stories for modern practitioners. The recognition on introspection may be a welcome respite from the frenetic pace of existence, offering a risk to slow down, take stock, and plan for the destiny.

Some human beings pick to have an fantastic time Alban Arthan in a communal way, collecting with like-minded individuals to proportion in rituals, feasting, and storytelling. These events frequently function a reminder of the interconnectedness of all matters and the price of community in darkish instances. In an generation in which many enjoy disconnected from nature and from every one-of-a-kind, the quiet reflected photo and communal togetherness that Alban Arthan can offer are greater precious than ever.

While the conventional additives of the competition won't generally align with present day life, its core necessities of rebirth, choice, and renewal are universally relevant. Whether you choose to maintain a solitary vigil, attend a network event, or certainly slight a candle in honor of the returning solar, the essence of Alban Arthan can provide a deeply full-size manner to navigate the complexities of present day existence.

Imbolc: The Promise of Spring

In the continuing exploration of the Druidic Wheel of the Year, we come to Imbolc, a opposition celebrated at the 1st or 2nd of February, relying on regional and cultural variations. This ancient opposition marks the halfway factor a few of the iciness solstice (Alban Arthan) and the spring equinox (Alban Eilir). Often visible because the promise of spring, Imbolc includes with it a experience of renewal, purification, and growing moderate. In this economic destroy, we can delve into the rituals, symbolism, and importance of Imbolc to understand how this competition need to enhance your contemporary lifestyles through its undying recognition.

Rituals and Traditions

The name Imbolc is notion to be derived from Old Irish, which means "within the stomach," which refers back to the pregnancy of ewes, a sign that spring is close to. In ancient times, Imbolc have become frequently associated with the fertility of the land, the promise of new lifestyles, and the awakening of the Earth after the deep sleep of iciness. During this competition, families might be very well cleaned, and antique assets can be cleared away, symbolizing the elimination of the vintage to make manner for the brand new. Hearth fires might be extinguished after which relit, invoking the spirit of renewal.

The Goddess Brigid, one of the maximum crucial deities inside the Celtic pantheon, is cautiously associated with Imbolc. Temples devoted to Brigid should host fires that had been stored burning at some stage in the period of the pageant. Specialized Priests and Priestesses, known as Flametenders, must maintain the ones fires as an offering for protection and blessings. Modern Druids often create a "Brigid's Cross" from reeds or straw, placing it close to their fireside or altar to ask Brigid's benefits into their houses.

Milk and dairy materials, symbolizing the lactation of the ewes, are conventional fare for the duration of Imbolc. Oat cakes, regularly prepared with symbolic shapes, are some different not unusual function. Modern practitioners additionally contain candlelit processions, poetry readings, and the crafting of "Brigid's beds"—small doll-like figures of the goddess—to honor this time of yr.

Symbolism of Imbolc

In Druidic cosmology, every of the festivals on the Wheel of the Year is cautiously tied to natural and cosmic occasions. Imbolc, especially, is aligned with the developing daytime and the warming of the Earth. The competition marks the stirrings of lifestyles beneath the floor of the land, symbolizing internal spiritual rebirth and private increase.

Snowdrops, one of the first flora to bloom as iciness wanes, are regularly associated with Imbolc. They are seemed as a promise that spring is truly on its way. Another symbol is the plough. In a few areas, embellished ploughs is probably led from door to door, with costumed youngsters following; offerings of food, cash, or drink were solicited, and in go back, blessings had been bestowed upon the homes and fields of the network.

Imbolc in the Modern Context

Today, many human beings find out the opposition of Imbolc to be an apt time for taking off new duties and placing intentions for non-public and spiritual growth. Just due to the fact the Earth prepares for a present day cycle of boom and rebirth, so too do humans experience the pull inside the path of renewal and transformation. Given the stresses of present day-day existence, the Imbolc season offers a danger to pause, replicate, and make conscious adjustments.

Practitioners regularly create altars decorated with white plants, candles, and emblems of Brigid. Journaling, meditative walks in nature, and dedicatory rituals are famous techniques to tune into the season's energies. Imbolc is likewise a time to start making plans your garden for the year, echoing the opposition's ancient agricultural roots. While metropolis dwellers might not have fields to plough or cattle to have a propensity, box gardening or maybe symbolic acts like planting herbs on a windowsill can deliver you towards the spirit of the season.

Alban Eilir: The Spring Equinox

Celebrating stability and fertility within the Druidic way of existence

The Spring Equinox, additionally called Alban Eilir in Druidic life-style, marks a time of balance among day and night time, slight and darkish. Occurring round March twentieth or 21st, this competition heralds the advent of spring, a season of growth, fertility, and renewal. In this financial disaster, we are able to delve into the symbolic significance of Alban Eilir, its ritualistic components, and the way current practitioners can include those historic practices into their lives for enrichment and stability.

Symbolism and Philosophical Underpinnings

The Spring Equinox serves as a instance of equilibrium and duality—standards which might be foundational in Druidic philosophy. The identical length of daylight and middle of the night throughout this period serves as a herbal example of stability, a rustic that Druids try to gather inner themselves and their environments. The season that follows, spring, symbolizes the rebirth and renewal of lifestyles, making Alban Eilir a competition of functionality and hope.

In Druidic concept, the Earth is taken into consideration as a dwelling entity, and spring is her time of blossoming and awakening after the extended iciness sleep. This is a season in which the natural global bursts right right into a palette of colors and a symphony of sounds, encouraging us to harmonize with the Earth's cycles. The stability struck on Alban Eilir a few of the forces of moderate and dark is not certainly an outside occurrence; it's also a call to find out this balance inner ourselves, to harmonize our very personal dualities and contradictions.

Chapter 4: The Fire Festival In Druidry

As we traverse the Druidic Wheel of the Year, the following huge competition we come across is Beltane. This competition marks the start of the warmer season and is positioned on the eve of the primary day of May, a time even as days increase longer and the Earth is alive with blossoming timber, flowering vegetation, and prolonged animal hobby. Beltane holds a unique vicinity within the Druidic calendar, as it's miles synonymous with fertility, hearth, and network bonding.

The Essence of Fire

Beltane receives its call from the Celtic god, Bel, which means "colourful one," and "teine," it's Gaelic for fireplace. Together, "Bel-teine" signifies "outstanding fireplace." Fire has been an essential detail for ancient civilizations, signifying not best warmth and light however moreover a purifying and invigorating power. The fires lit finally of Beltane serve more than one functions. First and critical, they may be concept to encourage the solar to live colourful and warmth in the path of the imminent season, facilitating crop growth and top harvest. Additionally, the fireplace serves as a image of purification and transformation.

Traditionally, big communal bonfires is probably lit on Beltane eve. The embers from the preceding 365 days's fireplace might be extinguished completely, marking a sparkling begin. The new fireplace became lit the usage of friction-based completely strategies, together with the fireside drill or flint and metallic. Once the hearth turned into ignited, it have become a hub for severa rituals. Animals would be herded among two fires to purify them, and it modified into considered correct proper fortune for younger couples to jump over the Beltane fireplace, hand in hand, to accumulate blessings of fertility and prosperity.

Symbols of Fertility and Union

Beltane celebrates fertility in its most expansive enjoy, not absolutely inside the context of human reproduction or agriculture however as a broader precept that could encompass creativity and one of a kind forms of growth and abundance. One of the most iconic symbols of this pageant is the Maypole. Traditionally, the Maypole is a tall wooden pole garlanded with greenery and plants, with extended ribbons associated close to the top. Participants, often an same extensive type of males and females, have to hold those ribbons and dance across the pole, weaving the ribbons in tricky styles. This dance is symbolic of the intertwining of the masculine and female energies, and the pole itself represents the Axis Mundi, or the area axis, which connects the heavens, the Earth, and the underworld.

Another ritual precise to Beltane involves the "Green Man," a figure embellished in foliage and green garments, representing the electricity and fecundity of nature. The

Green Man is a massive character in the festivities and is taken into consideration a spirit of the wooded place and flora. In a few rituals, people enact the symbolic union of the Green Man and the May Queen, a determine that represents the fertility of the Earth. This union embodies the sacred marriage of the God and Goddess, signifying the profound connection among the Earth and its populace.

Modern Adaptations and Community Involvement

In modern-day context, Beltane continues to be broadly celebrated amongst Druidic corporations, further to Wiccan and other neo-pagan traditions. While big public celebrations are not unusual, many humans moreover check this festival in non-public gatherings or solitary rituals. Contemporary practices may additionally consist of lighting fixtures a small fireside in a cauldron if a big bonfire isn't viable, decorating homes with flowers and greenery, and appearing individual fertility rites.

In addition to being a time of non secular and mystical observance, Beltane is likewise an occasion for network bonding. Potluck meals, crafting workshops, storytelling, and public performances are common sports. People frequently make "Beltane cakes," round-authentic baked items which are every now and then left as services for the Fae or elemental spirits.

Alban Hefin: The Summer Solstice

Understanding the Highest Point of the Sun's Journey

As we traverse the Druidic Wheel of the Year, we arrive at a celestial immoderate issue, every truly and metaphorically, referred to as the Summer Solstice or Alban Hefin within the Druidic manner of lifestyles. This competition celebrates the longest day and the shortest night time time of the one year, marking the zenith of the sun's annual journey. While Alban Hefin gives a time of exuberance and electricity, it also heralds the gradual descent into shorter days and growing nights. In this monetary catastrophe, we're going to delve into the spiritual, symbolic, and sensible factors of celebrating Alban Hefin inside the Druidic context.

The Cosmic Significance

The term "Alban Hefin" is derived from vintage Welsh words: "Alban" suggests "the slight of," and "Hefin" denotes "summer time." Together, they articulate the idea of the summer time mild at its pinnacle. In Druidic cosmology, the sun is often equated with a divine pressure, embodying the attributes of lifestyles-giving strength, enlightenment, and information. This aligns with many special global traditions that venerate the solar as a deity or image of divine impact. On at the prevailing time, the solar stands in spite of the truth that at its northernmost element, as observed from

Earth, before starting its flow lower returned adventure in the direction of the south. This stillness is visible as a second of deep cosmic stability, a time whilst the veil among brilliant worlds is thinnest, similar to at Samhuinn and Beltane.

The celestial phenomenon additionally correlates with Earthly cycles. Alban Hefin, the height of the solar's electricity, serves as a mirror to the natural global's power. Flowers bloom, animals are energetic, and the land is verdant. The sun fuels boom and sustains lifestyles, a reality that is decided and loved at some point of this time.

Rituals and Traditions

Many Druidic rituals for Alban Hefin revolve across the symbol of the Oak King, who represents the waxing 3 hundred and sixty five days, engaged in a legendary warfare with the Holly King, who symbolizes the waning year. At Alban Hefin, the Oak King is at the peak of his electricity however will fast relinquish his throne to the Holly King. Rituals also can incorporate the advent of an okaywreath, symbolizing the Oak King's crown, which is about alight in a managed fireplace to symbolize the sun at its zenith and the inevitable transition of power.

Bonfires are a common a part of the birthday celebration, serving as terrestrial mirrors to the celestial fireball that is the sun. Traditionally, herbs have been cast into the hearth as offerings to deities and spirits, and participants leapt over the smaller fires for achievement and purification. Many current Druids adapt the ones practices, likely deciding on green offerings and specializing in personal growth, network bonding, or environmental stewardship at some point of their hearth rituals.

The competition is also marked through celebrating the abundance of nature. Feasting isn't always unusual, with seasonal food that focus the Earth's bountiful offers. Song, dance, and storytelling are regularly included into the festivities, serving each amusement and ceremonial capabilities. Like one-of-a-kind festivals, the rites are tailored with the resource of way of humans and Druidic communities to suit their specific religious paths and geographical contexts.

Modern-Day Relevance

Today, on the same time as many people live disconnected from natural cycles, the Druidic party of Alban Hefin can function a awesome reminder of the interconnectedness of all lifestyles bureaucracy. For those feeling disconnected or spiritually adrift, this competition offers a grounding issue. It is a time to have a good time abundance but furthermore to mirror on the transitory nature of all subjects. The solar, at its maximum thing, has nowhere to head however down, education us the charge of savoring the instantaneous.

In modern exercise, Druids often increase the essence of Alban Hefin to embody a focus on environmental sustainability and community nicely-being. The light of attention is forged upon the shadow aspects of cutting-edge lifestyles—together with social inequality, environmental degradation, and the erosion of communal bonds. Celebrating Alban Hefin turns into an confirmation of moderate's electricity to mild up darkness, each metaphorically and in reality.

Lughnasadh: The First Harvest

The significance of thanking the Earth for her bounties

Lughnasadh, moreover spelled as Lammas, is a conventional Gaelic opposition that marks the start of the harvest season. It is one of the eight vital sabbats in the Druidic Wheel of the Year, typically celebrated round August 1st. This opposition isn't only a time for gathering ripened grains, end result, and veggies but additionally an occasion to honor the Earth for the bounty she has provided. In this financial ruin, we delve into the ancient roots, the symbolism, and the current-day interpretations of Lughnasadh, aiming to offer insights into how this historical Druidic practice can be meaningfully included into modern-day life.

Historical Roots and Significance

Lughnasadh is traditionally related to Lugh, a god from Irish mythology diagnosed for his skills in arts, crafts, and martial prowess. The pageant is stated to were initiated through Lugh as a funeral night meal in honor of his mom, Tailtiu, who died from exhaustion after clearing the plains of Ireland for agriculture. The ancient Druidic practices associated with Lughnasadh were geared toward ensuring a bountiful harvest and expressing gratitude to the Earth and deities for his or her gives.

The rituals frequently concerned the symbolic marriage of the god Lugh to the Earth goddess, signifying the union of masculine and female energies that create life. Games, athletic competitions, and artwork performances have been additionally applicable to Lughnasadh festivities, every as offerings to the gods and as a way to show the electricity and talents of the community.

Symbolism of Harvest and Gratitude

The topic of harvest is multi-layered in Druidic concept, extending past the literal collecting of grains to symbolize harvesting the non secular and emotional end cease end result of one's hard work in some unspecified time in the future of the three hundred and sixty five days. It is a time to mirror on the goals and aspirations you have got got cultivated and to assess what has come to fruition and what although requires nurturing. Just because the Earth's yield is cautiously harvested, measured, and stored for the approaching less warm months, Lughnasadh encourages the inner art work of comparing the 'harvests' of your very non-public life.

Gratitude, too, is a focal point within the path of this period. The idea isn't always virtually an emotional reaction however a deeply religious exercising. Druids historically provided the primary grains, culmination, and veggies to the gods and goddesses as a sign of gratitude and to secure divine pick out out for the the rest of the harvest season. In cutting-edge practice, this could arise as giving over again to the network or making aware efforts to understand the humans and times that have contributed for your 'harvest,' a few component form it is able to take.

Modern Interpretations and Practices

The historical customs surrounding Lughnasadh have stimulated a variety of contemporary practices. Many cutting-edge

Druids and pagans pick out out to mark this event via baking bread from the first grain harvest, after which ritually providing it in gratitude to the Earth or the usage of it in ritual feasts that embody pals and own family. Others can also hold ceremonies that contain the kindling of a ritual fireplace, symbolizing the transformative electricity of the Sun, which makes the harvest possible.

Revisiting athletic competitions and video video video games can be each other way to have a laugh this competition. While the actual competitions have been deeply tied to martial capabilities and bodily prowess, current video video games may be extra inclusive, which consist of organisation sports activities sports or highbrow video games, that consider collective intelligence and cooperation. Another frequent exercising is the crafting of corn dollies, complex designs made from straw, supposed to function a domestic for the spirit of the harvest thru the wintry climate months.

Alban Elfed: The Autumn Equinox

The Balancing Point

In astronomical terms, the equinox takes vicinity when the plane of Earth's equator passes through the middle of the Sun, ensuing in day and night time time being nearly the identical duration. For Druids, this event is an entire lot more than an insignificant calendrical footnote. It represents a non secular and mental balancing issue, reminding adherents to evaluate their very very own lives, deeds, and internal worldwide.

As the season transitions from summer time to autumn, the physical modifications within the surroundings are obvious. Leaves trade colour, days shorten, and a cooler air prevails. This is a time of harvest, of reaping what has been sown, each sincerely and metaphorically. The seeds of intention planted at the begin of the 12 months are actually bearing fruit. It's a period of thanksgiving however moreover a time for balance and pondered picture. How have your moves and options from earlier in the three hundred and sixty five days affected your contemporary situation? Are you preserving a harmonious stability between art work and relaxation, or social interactions and solitude?

Ritual Practices

Typical rituals for Alban Elfed embody services to the Earth, acknowledging the bounty it gives. This is commonly completed with the resource of sharing a feast with loved ones, with a part of the foods and drinks set aside as offerings for the Earth and the spirits of the area (genius loci). Altars may be decorated with acorns, pine cones, and autumnal leaves to symbolize the season. Some Druids moreover include corn dolls into their celebrations, representing the spirit of the grain. These dolls are regularly saved till the following planting season as a gesture to make certain future abundance.

Divination is a few other exercise that holds a particular resonance in the intervening time. The balance between light and dark makes it an auspicious time for attempting to find information concerning future endeavors or non secular paths. The equinox serves as a fulcrum, a problem of stability from which to endure in mind the unfolding destiny.

Modern Interpretations and Applications

In contemporary day speedy-paced, continuously-related world, the concept of stability may also additionally moreover appear old school or perhaps unimaginable. However, the standards embodied via Alban Elfed are universally relevant. Setting aside time for self-reflected photograph, despite the reality that only in brief, allows you to evaluate your existence's trajectory and make vital adjustments. The culture of giving thanks for the harvest can enlarge to showing gratitude for the emotional and non secular profits you have got made.

The workout of acknowledging and giving services to the Earth serves as a poignant reminder of our environmental obligations. As we gather nourishment and sustenance from the Earth, it's a gesture of reciprocity to offer again, be it thru sustainable dwelling, conservation efforts, or direct motion to shield herbal habitats.

In terms of personal improvement, the equinox serves as a properly timed reminder to try for balance in all elements of lifestyles—physical, emotional, and non secular. By listening to those dimensions and making small but extensive adjustments, viable attain a enjoy of equilibrium that isn't always handiest pleasant however also sustainable.

Chapter 5: The Role Of The Elements

Understanding the Importance of Earth, Air, Fire, and Water in Druidic Practices

The elements of Earth, Air, Fire, and Water have lengthy held large roles in Druidic philosophy and practices. They are considered the fundamental constructing blocks of the universe, interwoven into the very material of lifestyles. This financial ruin pursuits to discover how each of those factors is conceptualized in Druidry, their importance in ritualistic practices, and their broader implications for non-public growth and religious improvement.

The Elements in Druidic Philosophy

Druidic philosophy conceives of the factors as every literal and symbolic entities. Earth represents balance and material life; Air symbolizes mind, communique, and connection; Fire embodies transformation, electricity, and idea; and Water shows instinct, emotion, and the cyclical nature of life.

This conceptual framework frequently overlaps with different additives of Druidic notion, together with the Awen or the Wheel of the Year. For instance, unique gala's at some level inside the Druidic calendar are related to specific factors. Imbolc, the opposition celebrating the primary symptoms and signs and symptoms and symptoms of spring, is hooked up to the element of Fire, symbolizing the warm temperature that begins offevolved to interrupt wintry climate's icy grip. Lughnasadh, the pageant of the primary harvest, aligns with Earth, reflecting gratitude for the bounty provided via the land.

Ritualistic Involvement of the Elements

In Druidic rituals, the factors typically take middle degree. Typically, rituals begin with the 'calling of the quarters,' which incorporates invoking the factors to be discovered in each of the four cardinal instructions—North for Earth, East for Air, South for Fire, and West for Water. Each element may be invoked thru a combination of spoken word, gestures, or using ritual equipment which incorporates a wand for Air or a chalice for Water. Sometimes, representations of the factors, like a bowl of soil for Earth or a lit candle for Fire, are placed on an altar to function focal elements at some degree within the ritual.

The elements also play a role in purification internal rituals. Before enticing in the middle additives of a rite, individuals is probably 'swept' with an Air photo like a feather to cleanse them of mental clutter, or use water for purification of the spirit. Fire can be used symbolically to burn away impurities, every metaphorically via meditation or in reality via a small, managed blaze.

Personal Growth and Elemental Balancing

Understanding and appealing with the elements moreover provide avenues for non-public growth and spiritual improvement. In the Druidic way of existence, an imbalance among the factors inner a person should result in various forms of bodily or emotional misery. Someone with an excess of the Earth detail might be overly materialistic or stuck in inflexible styles, even as a deficiency in the Fire element have to take vicinity as a loss of motivation or low strength.

Conscious paintings with the elements can offer balance and wholeness. Meditation, ritual, or even lifestyle adjustments may be equipment on this enterprise. For instance, someone missing inside the Water detail can also additionally benefit from greater engagement with emotions thru journaling or counseling, at the same time as a deficiency in Air is probably redressed through taking over studies or carrying out intellectual debates.

Trees in Druidry

Exploring the Sacred Relationship Between Druids and Trees

Trees have constantly occupied a valuable feature in Druidry, forming the inspiration of severa rituals, mythologies, and spiritual mind. Considered to be the "fame humans" by the use of manner of Druids, timber provide knowledge, offer safe haven, and feature non secular symbols and conduits for energy. This bankruptcy delves into the tricky courting amongst Druids and wood, exploring how this bond manifests in various elements of Druidic practice.

The Symbolism of Trees in Druidic Beliefs

The importance of wood in Druidic ideals may be traced once more to historic instances, in which they were considered as sacred entities connecting the earth to the heavens. Each form of tree changed into concept to very very own precise attributes and tendencies, making them appropriate for distinct rituals and teachings. The Oak, for instance, has prolonged been associated with electricity, balance, and know-how. It is not any twist of fate that the word "Druid" is assumed to be derived from the Celtic words for alrightand data. Likewise, the Yew tree, often placed in ancient burial grounds, is attached with demise and rebirth, embodying the everlasting cycle of existence.

Trees moreover play an crucial feature inside the Ogham, an historic script utilized by the Druids, in which all of us corresponds to a specific tree or plant. This alphabetic system now not first-rate served as a manner of communique however additionally as a technique for divination. The Ogham is often hired in rituals to gain insights into one's life or to are looking for answers from the religious realm.

Trees in Rituals and Sacred Spaces

One cannot communicate Druidry without bringing up the essential feature that groves, or sacred forest clearings, play in the exercising. These sacred areas, regularly populated through some of wood, serve as meeting factors for Druidic rituals and gatherings. The desire of timber in the ones groves is intentional, geared towards growing a balanced power conducive to non secular paintings.

The act of tree planting is each different ritualistic workout deeply rooted in Druidry. This movement serves more than one skills: to expose reverence to the earth, to act as a form of environmental stewardship, and to set up a dwelling memorial or spiritual marker. It's an act that reverberates thru time, leaving an extended-lasting, living legacy.

Practical Ways to Engage with Trees

For modern-day Druids, enticing with wooden isn't solely reserved for formal rituals or gatherings. You can include tree understanding into your each day life through diverse manner. One not unusual practice is tree meditation, in which you connect to a tree to exchange strength and are seeking out expertise. Place your hands upon the trunk and recognition in your breath, permitting your energy to sync with that of the tree. Some Druids additionally acquire leaves, twigs, or bark (ethically sourced, of course) to create talismans or encompass them in altars.

Another manner to interact with timber is to have a have a look at their medicinal and realistic uses. Many Druids grow to be talented in herbalism, knowledge the restoration houses of diverse wood and the manner to harness them for both physical and religious nicely-being. For example, Willow bark has been used for its pain-relieving developments, at the same time because the Elder tree is frequently related to protection and recuperation spells.

Druidic Ritual Tools

Wands, Sickles, and Cauldrons: Understanding the Tools of the Druid

The mysticism of Druidry extends not high-quality to its philosophies and ceremonies but also to the physical devices that feature conduits for non secular electricity. In Druidic practices, device are taken into consideration greater than mere accessories. They are important to rituals, serving as mediums through which practitioners interest their intentions, hook up with the non secular realm, and perform severa magical and symbolic acts. This financial ruin delves into the significance, symbolism, and usage of key Druidic ritual gadget collectively with wands, sickles, and cauldrons.

Wands: Directing Spiritual Energies

In many magical traditions, wands are recognized as a essential tool for steerage electricity, and Druidry isn't any exception.

Traditionally, a Druidic wand is normal from the wooden of a tree that holds specific spiritual or magical importance. Oak, yew, and hazel are most of the maximum typically used varieties of wood. The crafting method itself is considered a spiritual task, frequently completed in the course of unique lunar levels and incorporating rituals that imbue the wand with the wielder's intentions.

Once crafted, the wand is consecrated thru ritual, rendering it an item of power. In Druidic ceremonies, it is often used to draw sacred symbols within the air, to delineate ceremonial place, or to direct energy toward a specific popularity. While the wand is normally related to the detail of Air, its attributes may be changed via diverse rituals to align it with exceptional factors or particular intentions. Given the wand's position in directing spiritual electricity, many Druids view it as an extension of their very non-public will and spiritual authority.

Sickles: Harvest and Transformation

The sickle holds a unique place in Druidic rituals, most extensively associated with harvest fairs like Lughnasadh. Unlike the wand, that may be a tool of projection and course, the sickle is a tool of transformation and transition. Its crescent form symbolizes cycles and stages, and it serves as an tool for reducing each bodily and metaphorically.

Traditionally, sickles are crafted from metal, regularly iron or bronze, and they'll characteristic complex designs or inscriptions that lend them specific attributes or powers. They are carried out in diverse harvest-associated rituals, now not fine for lowering flowers but moreover for symbolically "harvesting" the culmination of 1's hard work or the effects of one's intentions. The act of reducing with a sickle inside the path of a ritual can signify the severance of ties, the elimination of boundaries, or the marking of a change.

Given its symbolism, the sickle is likewise related to deities of harvest, transformation, and cycles.

Cauldrons: Vessels of Alchemy

The cauldron in Druidic life-style is a picture of abundance, transformation, and capacity. Its shape shows the womb of the Earth, making it a effective lady symbol. Cauldrons are typically crafted from metals like iron, bronze, or copper and can be embellished with relevant symbols or inscriptions. Their use in Druidic practices is manifold. They can also moreover maintain drinks applied in rituals, including water or mead, or function packing containers for burning herbs or services.

In ceremonies, the cauldron regularly represents the element of Water and is associated with functions like intuition, emotion, and receptivity. It's also a tool for alchemical transformation; factors added into the cauldron can be seen as elements of a spiritual or magical technique that transforms them into a few element new. Like the sickle, the cauldron is regularly associated with specific deities, especially goddesses related to the moon, fertility, and abundance.

Chapter 6: Sacred Geometry In Druidry

The Meaning and Use of Ogham and Other Sacred Symbols

Sacred geometry has been an essential part of non secular and religious practices during history, serving as a bridge a few of the cloth and spiritual worlds. Druidry, deeply rooted in the reverence for herbal methods and phenomena, moreover employs sacred geometry in its practices. This financial ruin delves into the significance of sacred geometry in Druidic rituals, with a focus on Ogham, an historic alphabetic script, and special pertinent symbols that find out resonance in Druidic lifestyle.

Ogham: The Celtic Tree Alphabet

Ogham is an archaic script used often for inscriptions positioned on status stones and in manuscripts. Its origins are shrouded in mystery, regardless of the reality that a few theories advise it superior from runic or Latin alphabets. Comprising a series of intersecting lines or notches and a stemline, Ogham's characters every represent a particular tree, making it deeply symbolic for Druids who revere bushes as sacred beings.

Ogham is extra than an insignificant alphabetic device; it is also a repository of historic information and symbolic meanings tied to each tree. For example, Birch (Beith in Ogham) is related to new beginnings, at the same time as Oak (Duir) symbolizes energy and stability. These symbolic meanings are regularly applied in meditation, divination, and rituals.

Ogham is occasionally employed for the casting of spells or the making of charms, etched into wood staves or stones. In present day-day Druidry, Ogham also can be used in divination much like Runes in Norse traditions. Practitioners can also moreover cast numerous Ogham staves or draw them randomly, interpreting the messages primarily based definitely truely on the tree symbolism and its importance inside the querent's life.

The Spiral and the Triskele

The spiral is a clean yet profoundly symbolic shape that appears in nature, art work, and religious symbolism global. For the Druids, the spiral can represent the path from outdoor hobby to the internal soul or the adventure from birth to loss of life and spiritual rebirth. Some historic Celtic carvings and stone circles include spirals in their layout, in addition cementing the image's significance.

Another image with a spiral-like form is the Triskele, or triple spiral. This logo has been determined in plenty of historical cultures however holds specific importance in Celtic way of lifestyles. The 3 fingers of the Triskele are idea to represent the tripartite department of the arena (Land, Sea, and Sky) or the cycle of lifestyles, loss of life, and rebirth. The Triskele's palms are equidistant, emphasizing the Druidic awareness on balance and concord amongst all topics.

The Pentacle and Sacred Geometry

Another form frequently related to Druidry is the pentacle, a 5-pointed star enclosed via a circle. Though extra commonly associated with Wiccan practices these days, the pentacle has roots in historic pagan traditions, consisting of these of the Celts. The five factors historically represent the four factors (Earth, Air, Fire, and Water) and Spirit, united by means of manner of the enclosing circle that symbolizes the connectedness of all lifestyles.

The pentacle is a extremely good example of sacred geometry, a concept that includes attributing symbolic meanings to fantastic geometric shapes and proportions. It's an age-vintage exercising, with echoes within the structure of historic pyramids, medieval cathedrals, and within the herbal international. While the term "sacred geometry" might also sound current, the idea has existed in severa paperwork for the duration of civilizations and time periods, which incorporates Druidry.

Sacred geometry in Druidry serves no longer most effective as an esoteric device of statistics but moreover as a realistic guide for ritualistic talents. The shapes and styles regularly maintain specific meanings and power signatures, which can be employed to direct electricity, interest reason, and create sacred spaces. For instance, laying out a pentacle pattern inside the route of a ritual may be a way to invoke elemental energies and foster a better connection with the natural international.

The Druidic Oracle

Animal Omens in Druidic Practice

In Druidic exercising, animals are not truly physical beings but are regularly considered messengers or representatives of the spiritual realm. The look, conduct, and motion of animals can bring particular meanings and messages. For instance, the crow, a hen related to magic and transformation, may need to symbolize alternate or the need for deeper insight right right into a scenario.

Animals encountered for the duration of meditation, desires, or bodily trips are also given remarkable significance. These "spirit animals" can provide understanding, protection, and steerage. To recognize the message of an animal omen, one has to bear in mind the context wherein the animal regarded, its stated symbolic that means, and any non-public institutions one may have with that particular animal.

For example, if a fox crosses your direction on the identical time as you are contemplating a complex situation, the traditional records should endorse which you could likely need to expect strategically or be cautious. Foxes are diagnosed for their cunning and intelligence. However, if you have a non-public revel in that links foxes to a awesome kind of statistics or message, that private symbolism is probably similarly valid.

Tree Omens and The Ogham

Trees are considerable to Druidic belief and exercise, serving as residing connections a number of the earth and the sky. Similar to animals, extraordinary tree species supply severa symbolic meanings, and their presence or specific dispositions can characteristic omens or messages. The Ogham, a Celtic script collectively with various strokes and features, is regularly applied in Druidry for divination, and every Ogham man or woman corresponds to a specific tree. The interpretation of those characters can be based clearly on the houses and conventional symbolism of the corresponding tree.

Divination strategies using Ogham frequently comprise casting a fixed of

Ogham staves—small sticks engraved with the characters—and interpreting the methods they land and their spatial relationships to every other. When casting Ogham staves, the reader considers the traditional meanings, the orientation of the staves, their proximity to every particular, and so on, to derive nuanced insights into the query or scenario reachable.

Druidic Divination Tools

Besides animal and tree omens, severa equipment may be hired for divination in Druidic practice. Runes, similar in characteristic to Ogham, are characters from runic alphabets utilized by the Germanic peoples. The casting of runes can provide insights into future sports or the person of specific conditions. Some Druids moreover hire the usage of crystals, pendulums, or possibly tarot playing cards which, despite the fact that no longer historically Druidic, may be tailored proper into a present day-day Druidic framework.

Divination equipment are commonly consecrated in a ritual placing, and the act of divination is regularly located by the use of prayers or invocations to deities, spirits, or the ancestors, requesting their steerage in decoding the symptoms and symptoms. The efficacy of those equipment isn't always honestly of their symbolism but inside the patron's potential to connect to better realms at the same time as the usage of them.

Druidic Chants and Songs

The Vibrational Aspect of Sound in Druidic Practices

Druidic philosophy posits that the entirety within the universe is interconnected through energy and vibrations. Chants and songs are believed to faucet into those vibrations, affecting every the religious and physical geographical regions. The tones, notes, and timbres in chants and songs are cautiously decided on for their vibrational features. According to Druidic beliefs, sure sounds resonate with precise elements, deities, or natural phenomena. For example, a low, rumbling tone is probably used to invoke the Earth element, whilst excessive, ethereal notes can be related to the detail of Air.

The vibrational difficulty of sound is vital to accomplishing the right state of thoughts during rituals. Specific melodies or sequences of notes are concept to align the individuals' energies, create an ecosystem conducive to religious exercise, and facilitate a connection with better powers or the natural worldwide. As individuals chant or sing collectively, they not only proportion the emotional and non secular experience however also attune their energies to the same frequency, enhancing the performance of the ritual.

Types of Chants and Songs in Druidic Ceremonies

In Druidic traditions, there are super sorts of chants and songs designed for various functions. Here are a few:

Invocation Chants: These are short phrases or sentences chanted in a repetitive way to call upon deities, elemental forces, or ancestors. The repetitive nature aids in inducing a trance-like country, making it easier to hook up with the invoked entity.

Narrative Songs: These are longer compositions that inform tales, generally of myths, legends, or historical activities super to the Druidic life-style. These songs serve each an academic and a ritualistic feature, maintaining lore and tradition at the same time as additionally channeling the spiritual energy of the testimonies they inform.

Mantras: While the term "mantra" is borrowed from Eastern non secular traditions, the idea exists in Druidry as well. These are commonly quick, powerful phrases designed to focus the thoughts and deepen religious expertise. Mantras in Druidic workout may be in Old Celtic languages or maybe in current English, reflecting the melding of historical records with modern-day exercise.

The preference of language for those chants and songs can variety widely. Some practitioners select out Old Celtic or Gaelic to honor the roots of Druidry, even as others decide on the usage of their close by language for a greater private connection. The cause and emotional resonance are taken into consideration more essential than the precise language used.

Practical Tips for Incorporating Chants and Songs

If you're new to incorporating chants and songs into your Druidic exercise, proper here are some steps to get you started out out:

1.   Start Simple: Begin with short, smooth-to-preserve in mind chants. You can

find many examples in Druidic literature or possibly create your personal based on what resonates with you.

2.   Be Mindful of Vibrations: Pay hobby to the tonal characteristics of your voice or devices if you're using them. Try to feel the vibration and modify as critical to benefit the desired emotional or spiritual usa.

3.   Group Dynamics: When chanting or creating a tune in a fixed, try to harmonize your voice with others, every in phrases of pitch and quantity, to create a unified sound and strength state of affairs.

four. Personalize: Feel unfastened to conform traditional chants and songs to better in shape your non-public beliefs or events. The maximum important element is the purpose and emotional resonance, now not strict adherence to conventional forms.

Chapter 7: Druidic Prayers And Invocations

How to Call Upon Deities, the Ancestors, and Elemental Forces

Druidic rituals and ceremonies are deeply interwoven with prayers and invocations. This spiritual language serves due to the fact the important link among the practitioner and the forces they are looking for to connect to—be it deities, ancestral spirits, or elemental energies. In Druidry, prayers and invocations now not handiest supply admire and devotion however additionally serve beneficial capabilities together with searching for guidance, protection, or benefits. In this financial ruin, we will delve into the forms of prayers and invocations utilized in Druidry, the protocols for their right use, and the way cutting-edge-day practitioners can adapt those historic workplace work for current goals.

Types of Prayers and Invocations in Druidry

1.   Invocation to the Deities: In Druidic practices, pretty some deities may be invoked, normally representing the herbal worldwide, celestial our our bodies, or forces of nature. For instance, the god Lugh is regularly invoked for talents and crafts, at the same time as the goddess Brigid is referred to as upon for recuperation and idea. The language utilized within the ones invocations is frequently poetic and rich in symbolism.

2.   Ancestor Veneration: Druids keep a deep understand for his or her ancestors, spotting them as assets of facts and steerage. Prayers and rituals often incorporate talking right away to the spirits of the ancestors, inquiring for their blessing, steerage, or assist.

three. Elemental Calls: One of the foundational factors of Druidry is the worship and recognize of the natural elements—Earth, Air, Fire, and Water. Invocations often start or surrender with a call to the ones elements, inviting them to participate in the ritual and bestow their precise abilities upon the complaints.

Proper Use and Protocol

Invocations and prayers aren't haphazardly thrown into Druidic rituals. The following are a few famous recommendations:

1.   Timing and Sequence: The time at which prayers and invocations are made regularly corresponds to specific ranges of a ritual or ceremony. For example, elemental calls is probably made at the start to set the level for the power work that follows.

2.   Direction and Posture: The course you face whilst making an invocation can also supply symbolic importance. Similarly, precise postures may be observed, such as repute with hands raised for calling the sky or kneeling to invoke the Earth.

3.   Articulation: The phrases need to be spoken absolutely, firmly, and with cause.

Mumbling or dashing thru an invocation may be visible as a signal of disrespect to the forces being referred to as upon.

Adapting Ancient Invocations for Modern Practice

The historic Druids left us with few written records in their prayers or invocations, which means that masses of what is used these days is a reconstruction or variant. Modern Druids frequently create their very non-public invocations based totally at the concepts and issue topics observed in ancient texts, folklore, and scholarly interpretations. The secret is to hold the spirit and rationale of the Druidic worldview at the equal time as making the language relevant for your non-public testimonies and understanding.

While it is important to be respectful and aware of the traditions, Druidry is also a residing, evolving path that invites private connection and interpretation. Whether you're writing your very personal invocations or adapting modern-day-day ones, your sincerity and intention are what actually depend.

The Druidic Concept of the Soul and Afterlife

Exploring Druidic beliefs about existence, dying, and rebirth.

The subject of the soul and the afterlife is shrouded in mystique and variety interior Druidic practices, similar to it's far in masses of one of a kind religious traditions. Druidry does now not very personal a completely unique, orthodox factor of view on these topics, but rather it gives pretty a range of insights derived from mythology, folklore, non secular evaluations, and individual interpretation. In this financial ruin, we are able to delve into the huge additives of ways Druidry perspectives the soul, existence after lack of life, and the cycle of rebirth.

The Nature of the Soul in Druidic Beliefs

The soul in Druidic knowledge is an immortal essence this is intrinsically related to the universe. Often seen as a microcosm of the divine or the universe, the soul is considered to be immanent—every inside us and in the global round us. While unique interpretations can range, many Druids adhere to the concept of animism, which posits that all matters—animals, plants, rocks, rivers, or maybe celestial our bodies much like the solar and moon—have a spirit or soul. This point of view fosters a profound revel in of interconnectedness with all styles of lifestyles.

Additionally, a few Druidic traditions find out the concept of the tripartite soul, a threefold branch comprising additives like idea, emotion, and power, now and again likened to the Celtic information of "Land, Sea, and Sky." This isn't a traditional perception amongst all Druids but is a fascinating lens thru which to find out the complexities of human life and the soul's multifaceted nature.

The Journey of the Soul and the Afterlife

Life after dying is every distinct place in which Druidry shows massive variety in concept. One commonplace concept is the "Otherworld," an alternate realm that souls journey to after death. This Otherworld is neither a heaven nor a hell however any other state of existence that is in element connected with our very personal worldwide. The Otherworld may be a place of rest and rejuvenation, in which the soul prepares for its subsequent life.

Another compelling detail of Druidic afterlife beliefs consists of ancestral veneration. The spirits of the ancestors are frequently believed to stay in the Otherworld and may be accessed thru ritual, meditation, or maybe smooth remembrance. In this experience, the road amongst this global and the subsequent is visible as permeable, considering interaction and mutual have an impact on. Some Druidic practitioners interact in ancestor worship as a manner of searching out steerage and understanding from those who've surpassed on earlier than them.

While the idea of reincarnation is not everyday in Druidry, it is quite everyday. The cycle of life, death, and rebirth is seen as a natural technique guided with the beneficial resource of the laws of the universe. Many Druids don't forget in some shape of reincarnation or transmigration of the soul, now not continuously confined to human office work. Some assume that souls may be reborn as animals, vegetation, or maybe factors, depending on the commands the soul wishes to investigate.

Ethical and Moral Implications

The Druidic perspectives at the soul and the afterlife may have profound ethical and moral implications. If the soul is eternal and linked to all lifestyles forms, it implies a nice diploma of obligation in the direction of not clearly fellow humans however additionally the environment and all residing beings. This view encourages a life of harmony, apprehend, and aware movement, all geared closer to each non-public and collective betterment. The concept of an ongoing relationship with the ancestors offers a ethical framework rooted in way of life and a recognize for the information of the beyond. Similarly, the perception in reincarnation can feature an ethical manual, as movements on this existence can also additionally moreover have repercussions in future lives.

Druidic Healing Practices

Using Herbs, Chants, and Energy Work for Physical and Spiritual Healing

Druidic practices, on the same time as rooted inside the traditions of the beyond, offer an array of herbal techniques to recuperation that may be blanketed into modern-day life. Druidic recovery encompasses bodily, emotional, and spiritual dimensions, and is based heavily on the understanding of the herbal global. In this financial ruin, we are able to delve into the primary components of Druidic healing, particularly using herbs, chants, and electricity art work.

Herbal Wisdom

Herbs play an vital function inside the recovery practices of Druidry, given their grounding in the Druidic reverence for the Earth and its bounty. From the usage of simple kitchen herbs like thyme and rosemary to extra specialized plants like mistletoe and hawthorn, the Druidic pharmacopeia is as numerous due to the fact the ecosystems from which it's miles sourced.

For instance, nettles is probably used for their excessive dietary cost and to treatment allergic reactions, at the same time as lavender is lauded for its calming houses and functionality to beneficial resource in sleep. Typically, herbs aren't simply ingested but also are employed in teas, salves, and ritual baths.

However, it is critical to be cautious and properly-informed at the identical time as the use of herbs, mainly for ingestion or topical software program. Not all plants are stable for human use, and man or woman hypersensitive reactions have to be considered. It is commonly recommended to go to healthcare specialists, especially in case you are pregnant, nursing, or beneath medication.

Chants and Songs

The Druidic tradition is replete with chants and songs used for numerous functions, which include restoration. They are frequently formulated the usage of the vibrational trends of sounds to resonate with the energies of the body and the natural global. The purpose is to create a harmonious drift of strength which can facilitate restoration, each via dispelling negativity or by means of invigorating the body's personal healing capacities.

One commonplace exercising is the use of vocalizations that mimic natural sounds, just like the rushing of water or the rustling of leaves, to connect the practitioner or patient to the energies of the Earth. These sounds can be integrated right into a ritual setting, concerning various factors like candles, crystals, or the casting of a circle, to beautify their restoration impact.

Energy Work

Energy artwork is some other pillar of Druidic recovery practices, frequently regarding arms-on techniques just like what's positioned in Reiki or Qi Gong. The principle underlying this approach is the perception that a life-pressure energy or

"Awen" flows thru all residing beings. Illness or ache is taken into consideration as a disruption or blockage on this go with the flow, and power art work dreams to repair it.

In a stylish recovery consultation, the healer may area their hands on or close to the affected character's frame, acting as a conduit for the restoration energy. Visualization strategies regularly accompany this exercising, helping both the healer and the affected person attention their purpose at the recovery technique. Sometimes, the resource of formality system like wands, staffs, or crystals can be used to channel the power greater efficaciously.

Druidry and the Community

How Druidic Principles Can Be Applied in Community Building and Social Justice

Druidry is not an isolated workout; it's deeply interconnected with the network and broader society. The statistics of

Druidry has a bargain to offer in phrases of making stronger, greater sustainable groups and promoting social justice. This bankruptcy delves into how Druidic thoughts may be woven into the cloth of present day network lifestyles.

Social Cohesion and Shared Values

Druidic philosophy places a immoderate fee on interconnectedness—of humans to each one-of-a-kind, to the Earth, and to all dwelling beings. This is clear in how Druid corporations feature. They are regularly closely-knit organizations that don't neglect the wheel of the three hundred and sixty five days collectively, percent assets, and look out for each exclusive. Applying this Druidic concept to larger societal structures, we discover a model for building social cohesion through shared values.

For instance, Druidic respect for nature can translate into community-primarily based totally environmental programs.

Communities must collectively have interaction in planting wooden, cleaning rivers, and maintaining close by parks, emulating the Druidic charge of stewardship of the Earth. Similarly, the fee of inclusiveness and equality in Druidry can encourage network tasks that cause for equal useful resource distribution or possibilities for all of us, irrespective of their records.

Community Rituals and Public Spaces

Public areas can be sanctuaries in which people come collectively to percentage, interact, and expand, similar to a Druidic grove. Initiating community rituals within the ones regions can be a effective way to bind humans collectively. Rituals might be as simple as monthly gatherings to have fun the modern-day day moon, seasonal gala's open to the overall public, or communal storytelling intervals that serve to pass on knowledge and foster a shared identification. The exercising of community rituals not simplest serves to strengthen social ties however furthermore features as a form of collective emotional and religious restoration, some element this is a lot wanted within the hustle and bustle of contemporary-day existence.

The Druidic apprehend for sacred internet web sites may additionally additionally encourage the network to regard public regions as 'sacred' in the enjoy that they may be vital for communal well-being. This mind-set should probable inspire higher protection, revolutionary enhancement, and extra thoughtful use of public areas, fostering a enjoy of shared ownership and understand among network members.

Druidry and Social Justice

The social justice factor of Druidry is deeply embedded in its middle values, in spite of the fact that it may now not usually be overtly said. The concept of interconnectedness inherently results in a sense of obligation toward folks that are marginalized or deprived. This translates right into a call for social justice, for making an attempt to stability the scales, and for community activism.

Druidry teaches that every one lifestyles is interconnected and that harming one harms the complete. This principle can pressure various social justice tasks, consisting of advocating for the rights of marginalized groups, taking component in environmental justice actions, or fighting in competition to systemic discrimination. As Druidry respects the sanctity of all life, it moreover compels its lovers to fight issues like animal cruelty and environmental degradation as forms of social injustice.

By taking the understanding of Druidry and applying it to trendy campaigns for social justice, you can imbue your activism with a deeper enjoy of motive and spirituality. This now not great enriches your very very own spiritual journey however additionally brings a completely particular, ethical, and prolonged-term attitude to social justice artwork.

Chapter 8: The Role Of Storytelling

The Significance of Myths, Legends, and Storytelling in Druidic Culture

Stories, myths, and legends had been on the middle of human subculture due to the fact time immemorial. In Druidry, storytelling serves as a tapestry that weaves together the complex aspects of nature, deities, non secular standards, and human research. Through the act of storytelling, Druidic practices move past past rituals and emblems to interact in a dynamic speak that resonates with the inherent narrative form of the universe. This bankruptcy targets to delve into the significance of storytelling in Druidry, its numerous office work, and the way it could be included into present day-day lifestyles.

The Archetypes and Life Lessons

Druidic stories regularly center round archetypes—traditional symbols that represent number one human studies.

These archetypes may additionally additionally encompass the Sage, the Warrior, the Mother, and so on. Each man or woman often serves as an allegory for better spiritual standards, schooling profound training which can be as relevant nowadays as they were masses of years in the beyond. For example, stories regarding the transformation of humans into trees or animals regularly communicate issues of empathy, harmony, and the interconnectedness of all lifestyles paperwork. These are not mere cautionary recollections or fables however deep philosophical commentaries designed to invite introspection and undertaking assumptions.

Besides presenting know-how, those recollections regularly feature a code of ethics, demonstrating thru the deeds of heroes and heroines the attributes of braveness, loyalty, and integrity. They provide a framework for what it way to be in concord with nature and other living beings. By focusing at the demanding situations and resolutions that characters stumble upon, the narratives serve as a blueprint for ethical and religious dwelling. For example, many Druidic memories speak the results of betraying the receive as proper with of a pal or network, dropping light on the significance of integrity and righteousness.

The Oral Tradition and Modern Interpretations

Traditionally, the ones memories have been handed down orally, from one technology to another, ensuring each the renovation and the evolving interpretation of the narrative. The oral way of life allowed for a more intimate and customized transmission of testimonies, as every storyteller may additionally need to add nuances or nearby flavors. This dynamic nature of storytelling in Druidic way of life makes it in particular wealthy and adaptable to fashionable contexts.

In cutting-edge day age of virtual media, the historical paintings of storytelling can appear preceding, but its requirements are pretty relevant. Modern Druids can hire numerous media, from books and podcasts to virtual paintings and movies, to relate the ones memories, drawing parallels amongst ancient consciousness and current demanding situations. While the medium has modified, the center precept of using narrative to preserve deep existential and ethical mind remains intact.

Integrating Storytelling into Modern Druidic Practices

Incorporating storytelling into one's Druidic exercising may be finished in myriad methods. One can begin via setting aside time for the duration of rituals or gatherings for the telling of conventional memories or private anecdotes that align with Druidic values. These recollections can be each a training tool and a form of entertainment, making the training greater memorable. Alternatively, storytelling may be individualized, in which one keeps a magazine to file goals, intuitive insights, or each day reflections. This workout can function a present day shape of 'bardic expression,' a way to find out and articulate one's non secular adventure inside the Druidic framework.

Druidry and Animal Guides

Understanding the Spiritual and Symbolic Importance of Animals in Druidry

In the Druidic way of existence, the natural international is seemed as a tapestry of interconnected beings, each one shielding a very specific importance and understanding. Among those, animals regularly have a unique location. They are seen as messengers, courses, and partners in the religious adventure, supplying insights which might be right away profound and elemental. This financial ruin delves into the importance of animal courses in Druidry, exploring their roles, significance, and the way to hook up with them in present day-day instances.

The Role of Animals in Celtic and Druidic Mythology

Animals aren't mere bystanders in Celtic and Druidic mythologies; they are active individuals or maybe catalysts for transformation. In many recollections, they feature courses or sentinels to other nation-states, revealing hidden truths or most important heroes to their destinies. For example, the Salmon of Wisdom is a well-known parent in Irish mythology, representing the last deliver of facts. Deer often constitute gentleness and intuition and are regularly related to goddesses of the land and forest. Birds much like the raven and eagle are considered messengers a number of the earthly and non secular geographical regions, embodying transformation and higher views.

The Druidic manner of life furthermore ascribes specific tendencies to specific animals, connecting them with the factors of Earth, Air, Fire, and Water. For instance, bears and boars are typically linked with the Earth, symbolizing groundedness and ferocity, respectively. Birds typically relate to the element of Air, embodying freedom and transcendence. Serpents and dragons, regardless of the fact that mythical, are related to the element of Fire, representing transformation and uncooked energy. Finally, aquatic animals like salmon or seals are associated with the Water element, symbolizing instinct and emotional depth.

Interpreting Animal Omens and Messages

The appearance of a selected animal to your life, whether or not or no longer physical or in desires, is often considered an omen or message in Druidry. It's essential to don't forget the context and your non-public feelings to interpret those encounters correctly. For example, if you again and again phrase a fox even as thinking of a complex situation, it might constitute the need for foxy and method. The conventional technique to understand such signs and signs and symptoms includes considering the animal's attributes, behavior, and characteristic in mythology. This frequently requires a mixture of have a examine, meditation, and intuition.

Connecting with an animal guide normally includes greater than a informal or unintentional assembly. It is a dating that develops over time, enriched through way of the usage of mutual respect and information. Some humans actively are seeking their animal guides thru meditation, shamanic visiting, or ritual, requesting steerage or insights into stressful conditions they will be dealing with. Others report that their animal guides regarded to them spontaneously, each within the physical international or thru visions and goals.

Integrating Animal Guides into Modern Practice

Modern Druids combine the information of animal publications thru incorporating their symbolism into rituals, meditations, and ordinary life. For example, you might use feathers, furs, or photographs of a particular animal in your altar to attract its strength and qualities. Some Druids additionally craft animal totems or amulets, imbuing them with the essence of the animal manual, to carry those energies with them. It is, but, crucial to approach this exercise with a sense of reverence and obligation. If using animal merchandise, try for moral sourcing to honor the spirit of the animal.

You can also hook up with animal publications through direct statement in nature, journaling approximately your encounters, and interpreting them for non-public insights. Even on the town environments, you may be aware birds, bugs, or mammals that frequent your surroundings. Each animal brings its very very own set of lessons and information. Observing them, studying their behavior, and meditating on their symbolic meanings can grow to be a satisfying a part of your religious workout.

The Druid's Cloak: Ritual Garb and Clothing

In the area of Druidic practices, ritual attire serves as greater than mere fabric that covers the body. It is a effective device that indicates a sacred space, represents the practitioner's cause, and aligns with the energies of nature and the factors. In this financial ruin, we delve into the symbolism and purpose at the back of the Druid's ritual garb, specifically focusing at the Druid's cloak, one of the most iconic and spiritually huge portions of clothing in Druidry.

Symbolism of the Druid's Cloak

The Druid's cloak is not only a garment but a picture steeped in manner of lifestyles and which means that. It often serves as a ritualistic boundary, enclosing the wearer in a sacred sphere and assisting within the transition from the mundane to the mystical realm. The colour of the cloak, whether or not it's miles white, inexperienced, or some other hue, frequently has unique significance. For example, white is normally associated with purity, spirituality, and the relationship to the higher self, even as green symbolizes the fertility of the Earth and a deep-rooted connection with nature. Some Druids even choose to beautify their cloaks with elements which includes animal furs, feathers, or maybe pieces of steel to represent severa totemic impacts or celestial our our bodies.

Fabric and Materials

The materials used to make the cloak are of equal significance. Traditionally, natural fibers like wool, linen, or cotton are desired as they maintain a closer connection to the Earth. Wool, being an animal-derived cloth, also can constitute concord with the animal nation. Some cutting-edge-day-day Druids, conscious of ethical problems, choose out sustainably sourced or recycled substances. The method of making the cloak can be a ritual in itself, with the weaver instilling it with goal and energy at each step. Custom-made cloaks can also include specific symbols, sigils, or even pockets to maintain ritual equipment or talismans, thereby enhancing the cloak's religious efficiency.

Guidelines for Wearing Ritual Garb

Though the Druid's cloak is possibly the most iconic, additionally it is a part of a broader set of formality garb that could encompass gowns, tunics, or possibly particular shoes. When taking element in agency rituals, a few orders have suggestions or traditions concerning what want to be worn. In many instances, the ritual attire is reserved absolutely for ceremonies, rituals, or meditation. However, solitary practitioners may adopt a greater personal and flexible technique to their ritual apparel, based mostly on their particular non secular wishes and expressions.

It's certainly nicely really worth noting that whilst the cloak and special quantities of formality clothing are powerful aids, they may be now not mandatory for the workout of Druidry. Many contemporary-day-day Druids select informal or normal clothing, deciding on as an opportunity to cognizance at the purpose and intellectual state added into the ritual. What's maximum vital is the practitioner's u . S . Of mind and openness to religious energies, in place of the appropriate clothing worn.

Chapter 9: Festive Foods And Drinks

What Foods and Beverages Are Significant in Druidic Celebrations

The culinary trouble of Druidic celebrations is greater than just a feast for the senses; it's far a communion with nature and a tribute to the Earth's abundance. In Druidry, the significance of foods and drinks extends some distance beyond smooth sustenance. These factors are considered sacred services, a way to honor the gods, the Earth, and the community. This chapter delves into the significance of meals and liquids in Druidic celebrations, detailing traditional dishes, their symbolism, and the way they may be protected into contemporary-day festivities.

Symbolic Foods and Their Significance

Many of the food applied in Druidic rituals and feasts have deep symbolic meanings, normally just like the season or competition being celebrated.

Grains: Especially critical throughout harvest gala's like Lughnasadh, grains like wheat, barley, and oats characterize the bounty of the Earth and the cycle of death and rebirth.

Fruits and Nuts: These are regularly used to honor the fertility of the Earth, especially in some unspecified time in the future of Beltane and Alban Hefin (Summer Solstice). Apples are particularly legit, associated with immortality and expertise.

Root Vegetables: Celebrated in the route of the much less heat months, root veggies like turnips and potatoes symbolize the hidden treasures of the Earth.

Dairy: Cream, milk, and cheese are related to abundance and are frequently blanketed in celebrations that honor fertility, on the side of Beltane.

Meats: Although Druidry encourages a respectful courting with all lifestyles paperwork, meat can be a part of the ritual feasting if it's miles sourced responsibly. It generally workplace paintings a part of the Samhuinn birthday celebration, symbolizing the sacrifice required for the survival of the community via the wintry weather months.

Sacred Drinks in Druidic Rituals

Drinks are not any less crucial in Druidic ceremonies, serving each symbolic and ritualistic abilities.

Mead: Made from fermented honey, mead is regularly utilized in rituals to honor the gods and goddesses. It is mainly famous in the course of Beltane and Midsummer celebrations.

Ale and Cider: These fermented liquids are not unusual in masses of Druidic gatherings, symbolizing every birthday party and the quit result of harvest.

Herbal Teas: Infusions of herbs like sage, thyme, and mint aren't handiest medicinal however additionally spiritual, frequently fed on for grounding and purification purposes.

Spring Water: The most effective of drinks, water, especially if sourced from a spring, is considered the essence of lifestyles and is utilized in purification rituals.

Modern Adaptations and Responsible Choices

Incorporating those traditional food and drinks into modern Druidic celebrations does not require strict adherence to ancient recipes. Many practitioners adapt the menu to in form their personal tastes, dietary restrictions, and ethical worries. Vegetarian and vegan alternatives are increasingly common, reflecting a modern-day sensibility in the route of sustainability and animal welfare.

When choosing substances, many Druids determine on domestically sourced, herbal, or straightforward-exchange alternatives to align with the Druidic precept of residing in concord with the Earth. It's now not pretty a great deal what you eat but how your alternatives effect the planet and its population.

Crafting Druidic Rituals

A Step-thru-step Guide to Creating Your Own Druidic Rituals

In Druidry, rituals are considered essential religious tools that facilitate connection with the divine, nature, and the network. Though there are set up ceremonies for severa fairs and events, there may be moreover considerable room for personalisation. Crafting your very very personal Druidic rituals may be a profitable revel in, permitting you to fully immerse yourself within the religious path and make it uniquely yours. This chapter objectives to provide a step-by the usage of-step manual to developing your very very own rituals, breaking down the fundamental additives and explaining a way to piece them together cohesively.

Understanding the Basic Structure

Before diving into the data of crafting your ritual, it's far important to understand the underlying shape that office work the skeleton of maximum Druidic rituals:

1.	Purification: Before beginning any ritual, it's miles essential to cleanse the distance and the participants. This may be finished thru smudging, asperging (sprinkling water), or some different approach to do away with horrible electricity.

2.	Invocation: The next step is to name upon the forces you need to ask into your ritual. This also can encompass the elements, ancestors, deities, or spirit courses.

3.	Main Working: This is the coronary heart of the ritual in which you carry out the sports necessary in your ritual's reason, in conjunction with meditation, spellwork, divination, or advantages.

four. Offerings and Thanks: It is vital to expose gratitude to the forces and entities that you've known as upon. This can be accomplished through presenting food, drink, or a few other present as a token of your appreciation.

5. Closing: Finally, the ritual is concluded via the usage of thanking the forces that have been invoked and disregarding them gracefully, ensuring that no non secular "doors" are left ajar.

Crafting the Core Components

1. Defining the Purpose: The first actual step is to determine what you want to perform. Whether it's miles for religious growth, recuperation, or celebrating a competition, the purpose will guide every subsequent selection in the crafting method.

2.   Setting and Tools: Decide wherein the ritual will take vicinity and what gadget you may require. Make extraordinary to bear in mind the elements you may be jogging with and pick a placing and gadget that align at the side of your reason.

three. Script and Sequence: Write down what you endorse to say and do. This may not need to be a inflexible script; it may characteristic a manual. Sequence the sports regular with the fundamental shape referred to above.

four. Choosing Invocations and Offerings: Depending on your purpose and the entities you are invoking, tailor your prayers, chants, and offerings. Make amazing they will be respectful and aligned with the traditions and energies you're going for walks with.

5.   Rehearsal: Before the real ritual, it's miles continually an wonderful concept to do a exercise session to ensure the whole thing flows without troubles. This is

specifically important if you are consisting of diverse participants.

6.   Execution and Record-Keeping: Perform the ritual as deliberate and make certain to file your studies. This now not most effective serves as a treasured pondered photo however also can provide insights for destiny rituals.

Tips for Personalization

1.   Incorporate Personal Symbols: Personal or family symbols can be included to characteristic a layer of private which means that.

2.   Music and Chants: Use music or chants that resonate with you. These can uplift the non secular environment and make the enjoy greater profound.

3.   Involvement of Others: Depending for your consolation stage, incorporate own family or network individuals who

percentage your Druidic course. This ought to make the ritual stronger and communal.

four. Blend with Other Practices: If you are eclectic on your spiritual course, you may choose out to encompass factors from other traditions, so long as they do no longer warfare with the center Druidic requirements and the ritual's motive.

Crafting your personal Druidic rituals is a profound way to deepen your spiritual workout, connect with nature, and locate balance in your existence. By expertise the easy shape, honing in on the ritual's motive, deciding on the right putting and tool, and such as private elements, you may create a wealthy tapestry of vast evaluations. The act of personalizing rituals permits you to embed your energy and motive into the exercising, making each ritual a very precise and transformative experience. Whether you are new to Druidry or an professional practitioner, the approach of formality crafting gives endless possibilities for spiritual exploration and growth.

Chapter 10: Energy Work And Meditation

Techniques for Grounding and Channeling Energy in Druidic Practices

Druidic practices regularly require a deeper connection to the factors, the Earth, and the spiritual worldwide. Achieving this isn't always clearly a remember of enacting rituals or memorizing chants, however moreover entails precise paintings with the energies round us. In this financial ruin, we can delve into pivotal elements of Druidic exercising: energy paintings and meditation. Both serve to ground the practitioner and permit for a more profound experience all through rituals, divination, or maybe every day activities.

Grounding Techniques in Druidry

Grounding is essential for each person operating with energies, specifically within the course of religious practices. It lets in you to anchor your energy to the Earth, supplying a sturdy foundation for any ritualistic or meditative art work. Grounding strategies variety, but the core idea is generally the equal: connecting your electricity to the Earth to create stability and stability. Here are some famous strategies:

1.   Rooting: Visualize your ft developing roots that penetrate deep into the Earth. Imagine the ones roots drawing energy up into your body, filling you with existence force. This may be executed even as reputation or sitting.

2.   Tree Emulation: Druids have a completely unique affinity for wooden. Stand or take a seat down, visualizing your self as a tree. Feel your roots anchoring you, your trunk supplying balance, and your leaves interacting with the factors. This approach may be very powerful, in particular while practiced outdoors.

three. Stone Anchoring: If you are interior or cannot visualize efficiently, protecting a grounding stone like hematite, tourmaline, or even a handful of soil can help facilitate the grounding approach.

These techniques function preparation for rituals, spells, or maybe normal existence, permitting you to address energies greater efficaciously. Grounding allows in draining away extra energy, emotional imbalances, or strain, supplying a easy slate upon which you may paintings.

Meditation and Mindfulness in Druidry

Meditation is some different tool for balancing the thoughts and spirit, enriching each your every day lifestyles and non secular practices. While meditation in the context of Druidry isn't always identical to practices in different traditions like Buddhism or Hinduism, the center desires are comparable: mindfulness, presence, and tranquility. A few Druidic meditation techniques embody:

1.   Elemental Meditation: This involves sitting in a quiet space and focusing your thoughts on one of the elements—Earth, Air, Fire, or Water. Visualize and experience its inclinations and its relationship together with your body and spirit.

2.   Journeying: This method is a shape of guided meditation in which you project into an imagined sacred landscape. The purpose is to speak with non secular entities, together with gods, ancestors, or animal spirits, and advantage know-how or notion.

three. Awen Meditation: Awen, as discussed in Chapter four, is the divine concept in Druidry. Meditating in this concept can offer readability, creativity, and a deeper connection to the non secular worldwide.

Balancing Energies

Both grounding and meditation serve to balance energies inside the practitioner. While grounding focuses on your connection with the Earth, meditation permits in aligning your internal energies. Both those strategies are particularly useful earlier than and after a ritual to balance the power go with the flow, however they're additionally useful in regular lifestyles for coping with pressure, making choices, or truly connecting with nature on a deeper stage.

Sacred Dance and Movement

The Role of Physical Expression in Ritual and Worship

The richness of Druidic practices isn't restrained to verbal expressions, rituals, and the use of sacred tools. An regularly neglected however crucial element of Druidic spirituality is the usage of the body as a vessel for divine energies and as a manner to hook up with the herbal global. Sacred dance and movement serve this cause well, growing a sensory channel for experiencing the energies of the factors, the divine, and the surrounding surroundings. In this bankruptcy, we will delve into the feature that sacred dance and movement play in Druidic workout, studying their ancient roots, typologies, and the manner one would probably comprise them into modern-day-day practices.

Historical Context of Dance and Movement in Druidry

In historical times, Celtic and Druidic societies associated awesome significance to bop and motion, often integrating them into their rituals, gala's, and ordinary life. While the specifics can be elusive due to the oral nature of Druidic traditions and the scant historical facts, it's miles widely believed that dances had been executed to honor deities, to have an excellent time the cycles of nature, and to mark rites of passage. There are many money owed of ring dances, spiral dances, and different formations that have ritualistic implications. These dances had been frequently accompanied with the resource of the usage of drums, flutes, and one-of-a-kind gadgets, growing a multisensory ritualistic experience.

While the Celts and Druids won't have had a formalized system of sacred dance, the actions completed had been whole of symbolism and imbued with purpose. For example, the spiral dance, frequently performed at gala's like Beltane and Samhain, symbolizes the eternal cycles of shipping, dying, and rebirth. The ring dance, typically executed in a circle, can constitute concord and the interconnectedness of all lifestyles paperwork.

Typologies of Sacred Movement in Modern Druidry

In the contemporary context, Druidic practitioners frequently include three critical types of sacred movement into their rituals:

1.   Purification Movements: These are often easy, repetitious movements finished

at the beginning of a ritual. The reason is to enter a meditative state and to purify the spiritual area. Simple actions together with sweeping motions, or even more complicated dance patterns designed to imitate the elements, can be used proper right here.

2. Energetic Movements: These are energetic, often rapid-paced actions that cause to elevate energy throughout a ritual. They are supposed to evoke the frame and thoughts and to music into the energies of the Earth and the divine. The steps and motions may be stimulated via way of animal actions, natural phenomena, or symbolic shapes similar to the spiral or circle.

3. Meditative Movements: These are slow, deliberate actions that goal to instill a enjoy of tranquility and connection. They are normally executed in the direction of the stop of a ritual to assist floor the

electricity raised and to put together for the remaining of the sacred region.

Incorporating Sacred Dance and Movement into Your Practice

Even if you take into account your self a amateur inside the realm of dance, the beauty of sacred motion is that it does no longer require formal training. Instead, it needs a willingness to hook up with your frame and the energies round you. Here are a few steps to start integrating sacred dance into your Druidic practices:

1.   Start Simple: Even clean arm and hand moves, while finished with intention, may be powerful.

2.   Seek Inspiration: Look to the natural international, conventional Celtic dances, or perhaps exceptional non secular practices for motion mind.

three. Use Music: While not strictly vital, track can notably beautify the enjoy of sacred dance.

four. Integrate into Existing Rituals: You can with out problems contain movement into your Druidic celebrations of the Wheel of the Year, your rites of passage, or your each day devotional practices.

five. Practice with Others: If feasible, sporting out group dance can be pretty effective, as the generated electricity is magnified through collective goal.

Druidic Groups and Orders

Exploring the Various Druidic Organizations and Finding One That Aligns With Your Beliefs

The pathway of Druidry is flexible and accommodating of various man or woman options and ideals. Whether you're genuinely starting out or looking to deepen your practice, turning into a member of a

Druidic corporation or order can offer both steering and network. These agencies can also feature the custodians of historical understanding, bridging the distance among historical Druidry and its modern variations. In this financial ruin, we're able to discover numerous sorts of Druidic businesses and orders, delve into what you can anticipate whilst taking part in those businesses, and offer guidelines for finding an commercial enterprise employer that aligns properly along side your very very own non secular aspirations.

Types of Druidic Organizations

Druidic groups often vary in recognition, structure, and guiding ideas. However, they commonly fall into one of the following lessons:

1.	Druid Orders: These are formal organizations often with a hierarchical form similar to that of traditional Druidic societies. They can also furthermore offer graded teachings, formal initiation ceremonies, or perhaps their personal interpretation of Druidic philosophy and formality. Well-acknowledged Druid orders may additionally moreover have global branches and a massive community of fans.

2.   Grove Circles: Groves are smaller, nearby gatherings of Druids. Unlike orders, they will not have a strictly described hierarchical shape. The emphasis in a grove is commonly on network, seasonal celebrations, and shared reading. Some groves are affiliated with larger orders, whilst others carry out independently.

three. Online Communities: In the virtual age, many Druidic practitioners discover network via on-line systems. While those lack the in-man or woman ritual and active exchange, they provide get entry to to a wealth of information and a miles broader, worldwide community of like-minded humans.

What to Expect

Philosophy and Teachings

Different Druidic agencies have particular techniques to Druidry, inspired via the use of their historic lineage, founding standards, and geographical origins. Some may additionally align cautiously with Celtic spirituality, emphasizing gods and goddesses from Celtic pantheons, at the same time as others may also moreover take an eclectic technique, incorporating various religious traditions.

Rituals and Celebrations

Organizations can also have particular tactics of celebrating the Wheel of the Year, the lunar cycles, and distinct key Druidic festivals. While there is normally room for personal expression, advantageous orders may also additionally prescribe unique rites, prayers, or ceremonial apparel for those sports.

Community Involvement

Community engagement varies from institution to employer. While some groves and orders are quite involved in public rituals, academic workshops, and ecological sports, others are extra insular and consciousness often on non secular improvement among their current individuals.

Finding the Right Fit

1.   Do Your Research: Begin via analyzing the challenge statements, philosophies, and sports activities of numerous companies. Look for on-line opinions or testimonials, if to be had.

2.   Attend Open Events: Many groups host public rituals or open conferences. These can provide a tangible experience of the agency's dynamics, practices, and network ethos.

3.   Talk to Members: Engaging in conversations with cutting-edge-day individuals can offer beneficial insights into the ordinary functioning and the lived experience of being part of that enterprise enterprise.

four. Trust Your Intuition: Your gut feeling about a fixed is great. If you sense comfortable and stimulated, opportunities are it's a terrific healthy for you.

five. Commitment Level: Understand the quantity of dedication anticipated via the organisation. Some organizations require regular attendance and development via educational publications, at the same time as others are extra snug.

To sum up, Druidic companies offer various philosophies, community systems, and practices. Whether you're attracted to the formality of a longtime order, the intimacy of a nearby grove, or the power of on-line organizations, there is probably a set that fits your very non-public non secular leanings and aspirations. Taking the time to discover those options can boom your exercise, provide a experience of community, and provide greater assets for getting to know and non secular boom.

Solo vs. Group Practice

The Pros and Cons of Practicing Druidry Alone or in a Community

Druidry, with its tough tapestry of philosophy, rituals, and traditions, offers a massive number of pathways for spiritual seekers. Some discover solace and enrichment running toward on my own, some distance from the complications of employer dynamics. Others thrive within the community placing of a Druidic grove or order, wherein shared rituals and collective understanding decorate their experience. This economic damage explores the advantages and annoying conditions of each approaches, that will help you make an knowledgeable choice that aligns along with your precise desires and aspirations.

Solo Practice: The Path of Individualism

Advantages

1.   Personal Freedom: Practicing solo lets in you the strength to conform rituals, traditions, and philosophies to suit your particular angle. There isn't any group consensus you should adhere to, leaving you unfastened to discover special sides of Druidry at your very very very own pace.

2.   Deep Self-Reflection: Without the distraction or have an impact on of a difficult and speedy, you may immerse your self greater deeply in introspective practices which encompass meditation, prayer, and divination. This regularly lets in for a extra nuanced information of self.

three. Schedule Flexibility: Solo exercising way you could examine Druidic vacations, meditations, and rituals on every occasion it's miles most on hand for you. You're not tied to the schedules of others, that is specifically useful for people with irregular work hours or circle of relatives commitments.

Challenges

1. Isolation: The drawback of the shortage of network is the absence of shared experience and out of doors perspectives, that would bring about a sense of isolation.

2. Limited Guidance: Without the form of a set or mentors, the adventure must emerge as overwhelming. There is a threat of misinterpretation or incomplete knowledge of complicated Druidic thoughts.

three. Self-Motivation Required: The absence of network duty technique that the impetus for everyday practice and take a look at rests mostly on you, which may be hard for some humans.

Group Practice: The Community Connection

Advantages

1.   Collective Wisdom: A group putting offers a wealth of enjoy and views which you can now not stumble upon otherwise. Learning from others can offer shortcuts for your personal facts and growth.

2.   Shared Energy: Many find out that rituals and ceremonies are stronger while achieved as part of a group. The collective popularity and intent can enlarge the non secular experience.

3.   Emotional and Spiritual Support: Being a part of a community approach you've got were given were given a community of like-minded people for steerage and resource. During difficult times, this will be a useful resource.

Challenges

1.   Group Dynamics: Personalities can clash, and internal politics can become a

distraction from the number one spiritual recognition of Druidry.

2.   Commitment: Most businesses have scheduled meetings, rituals, and different sports activities that you'll be expected to wait, which may not usually align along with your non-public time table or commitments.

three. Standardization: In a hard and rapid, there can be often a standardized manner of task rituals and interpreting doctrine. This have to enjoy limiting if you are someone who loves to discover or modify conventional strategies.

Chapter 11: The Druidic Path For Children And Families

The teachings and knowledge of Druidry aren't limited to a specific age company or demographic; they offer profound insights and steering for human beings at any degree of existence. This includes kids and families, for whom Druidic practices can feature precious resources for non-public development, ethical grounding, and the building of familial bonds. This economic catastrophe explores how the Druidic route can be adapted for extra more youthful generations and the way families can collectively interact with those historic practices to enhance their each day lives.

Introducing Druidry to Children

The Druidic direction is wealthy in storytelling, nature-based totally absolutely sports, and rituals that could captivate the imagination of kids. When introducing Druidry to younger own family individuals, preserve in mind beginning with engaging testimonies from Celtic mythology. These memories are not simply interesting; further they convey ethical and moral lessons which can help shape a little one's worldview. For instance, testimonies of heroes and heroines overcoming traumatic conditions with wit, braveness, and honor can feature valuable existence commands.

Incorporate nature walks and outdoor sports activities into your family's routine. Druidry places a robust emphasis at the reverence of nature, and there's no better manner to instill this charge in kids than with the useful useful resource of supporting them expand a personal courting with the natural worldwide. Whether it's a hike inside the woods, planting a garden, or without a doubt looking at the changing seasons, those sports provide first-rate opportunities for education youngsters about the interconnectedness of all existence and the importance of environmental stewardship.

Family Rituals and Celebrations

One of the extra massive components of Druidry is the Wheel of the Year—8 seasonal fairs that mark the herbal cycles of the Earth. These can be outstanding sports for circle of relatives gatherings and rituals. For instance, for the duration of Beltane, households can assemble a small hearth to have amusing the move decrease returned of heat and slight. During Samhuinn, do not forget growing a family ancestral altar to don't forget and honor deceased family members. The act of accumulating collectively for such rituals no longer simplest enriches the non secular lives of each family member but also strengthens familial bonds.

Crafting a circle of relatives ritual need no longer be complex. The essence lies inside the intention and the communal engagement within the act. Family rituals can variety from announcing a Druidic prayer in advance than food to protecting a more complex rite in the course of one of the 8 festivals. What is vital is that every member of the family feels covered and associated in the path of these sports.

Ethical and Moral Foundations

Druidry offers a robust framework for growing moral and ethical character. Central to Druidic philosophy is the idea of stability and concord, now not truly with nature however additionally in a single's social interactions. Concepts like justice, integrity, and admire for all types of lifestyles may be easily integrated into every day family discussions and choice-making techniques.

Parents can use the Druidic reverence for all life bureaucracy to instill in youngsters a enjoy of empathy and compassion. Discussions approximately the sacredness of timber, animals, or perhaps stones can amplify a toddler's understanding of the importance of kindness and fairness not just in the route of people but additionally to all beings. Additionally, the Druidic perception in the interconnectedness of lifestyles and the cycles of beginning, lack of lifestyles, and rebirth can assist kids address problems which encompass loss and alternate, presenting them a broader thoughts-set on the stressful conditions and transitions of existence.

Modern Challenges and Controversies

While Druidry is an historical religious route with a good deal knowledge to provide, it is not with out its stressful conditions and controversies, particularly inside the present day context. This financial disaster goals to talk approximately the complexities Druidry faces these days, which incorporates problems of cultural appropriation, environmental sustainability, and the manner it interfaces with current generation and social media.

Cultural Appropriation and Authenticity

One of the maximum contentious troubles in contemporary-day Druidry is the accusation of cultural appropriation. Since modern-day Druidry attracts carefully from Celtic traditions, it increases questions on who has the "proper" to workout and interpret these traditions. Some argue that non-Celtic humans carrying out Druidry is probably appropriating a way of life that is not theirs. This is in addition complex by the truth that cutting-edge Druidry is an amalgam of various sources, no longer absolutely rooted in historical authenticity. Therefore, it could be tough to determine what constitutes real Druidic exercise and who gets to make that name.

The notion of "authenticity" is itself a topic of debate. Historical Druids left inside the back of just a few statistics, and lots of what we recognize approximately them comes from Roman debts, which can be biased. Thus, current-day practitioners regularly depend on a mixture of scholarly studies, personal gnosis, and network consensus, leaving room for interpretation and capability disagreements.

Environmental Concerns

Given that nature reverence is a cornerstone of Druidic philosophy, the motion faces annoying conditions associated with environmental sustainability. While the manner of existence emphasizes a harmonious courting with the Earth, the practicalities of residing in a modern-day, industrialized worldwide may additionally need to make this tough. For instance, using ritual tools made from natural substances like timber, stone, or animal factors can increase ethical questions, particularly if those materials are not sourced sustainably. The catch 22 situation extends to the choice of foods and drinks in rituals and fairs, similarly to the environmental effect of gathering in sacred herbal websites, which may be bothered via human intrusion and littering.

Moreover, the wider challenge for Druidry, as for any nature-focused spirituality, is to move beyond individual or ritualized expressions of Earth reverence to greater huge, impactful environmental activism. The hazard of climate change, habitat loss, and species extinction makes this a urgent difficulty that Druidic businesses cannot find the cash for to disregard.

Technology and Social Media

In an generation dominated thru digital technology and social media, Druidry faces the challenge of maintaining its essence as a nature-based totally religious direction. On one hand, on-line systems offer the community excellent possibilities for connection, studying, and dissemination of information. Virtual groves and forums make the way of life to be had to folks that would probably in any other case be geographically or socially remoted. Online publications and belongings provide avenues for deepening one's facts of Druidic philosophy and exercise.

On the alternative hand, this technological engagement risks diluting the direct, experiential connection to nature that is important for Druidic spirituality. There is a problem that the critical sensory and physical elements of the tradition, like the sensation of the earth beneath one's feet or the sound of a stream, could be overshadowed with the resource of a digital revel in. Additionally, the commodification of spirituality on social media—where the focus would possibly probably shift to aesthetic representations of rituals or sacred web sites as opposed to their intrinsic fee—can detract from the intensity and sincerity of the exercising.

Chapter 12: Lifelong Learning And Spiritual Growth

The Druidic course is an evolving adventure that encompasses not certainly a fixed of rituals and philosophies, however a holistic way of life. As with any spiritual or non secular way of life, the journey is in no way in truth whole. There is typically room for in addition exploration, improvement, and deepening of information. In this concluding chapter, we can talk avenues for lifelong reading and religious boom interior Druidry, touching upon continued education, mentorship, and the workout of each day rituals as technique to foster an extended-lasting relationship with the historical data of Druidry.

Continued Education and Study

One of the essential trouble components to lifelong boom within the Druidic path is sustained education. Unlike many installation religions, Druidry does no longer provide a single, unchanging doctrine but encourages personal exploration and test. Here are some strategies you can preserve to supplement your records:

1. Advanced Courses and Retreats: Many Druidic companies provide superior courses that pass past the fundamentals. These might in all likelihood delve into the nuances of formality exercise, the Ogham alphabet, or Druidic statistics in extra depth. Retreats, often held at sacred internet net sites, offer immersive studies.

2. Reading and Research: With the abundance of books, educational papers, and on-line assets to be had, self-take a look at is a as a substitute possible path. While earlier works may additionally additionally additionally provide foundational expertise, more moderen works can offer easy views or specific interpretations of Druidic requirements.

three. Interdisciplinary Studies: Druidry has intersections with severa disciplines which includes ecology, Celtic studies, and comparative faith. A broader understanding of these areas can boom your Druidic practices and views.

Mentorship and Community Involvement

Mentorship is every other powerful street for spiritual increase. Learning from a person who has walked the path in advance than you may provide insights which may be hard to return via through solitary exercising or studying. Becoming a mentor after gaining enough experience can also deepen your knowledge and satisfy the offer-and-take philosophy it truely is not uncommon in lots of spiritual traditions.

Community involvement offers a few different layer of intensity for your exercise. By venture organization rituals, taking thing in network service, or maybe taking over a management function on your Druidic community, you make contributions to the collective understanding and moreover take a look at from the diverse practices and perspectives that others deliver to the table.

Daily Rituals and Mindfulness Practices

Lifelong learning and non secular increase in Druidry aren't confined to formal schooling or community involvement. They moreover stand up in the every day rituals and mindfulness practices which you comprise into your manner of life. A consistent practice can feature a non-prevent shape of non secular nourishment. This may be as smooth as a morning meditation focusing on the factors, a mid-day walk in nature, or an night gratitude ritual. Over time, these each day touchpoints turn out to be the underpinning of a lived Druidic philosophy, contributing to a lifelong exercising.

Chapter 13: The History Of Druidism

In delving into the depths of the beyond, we discover the rich tapestry this is the records of Druidism. This historical lifestyle, steeped in thriller and reverence for the herbal worldwide, holds a extremely good place in the annals of human religious exploration. To recognize the origins of Druidism, it's far critical to transport ourselves lower lower back to the depths of time, to a duration referred to as the Iron Age. It is right here, a number of the luxurious landscapes of what we now name the British Isles and elements of continental Europe, that the seeds of this magical exercising have been sown. The etymology of the phrase 'Druidism' itself exhibits a good buy approximately its essence. Derived from the Old Irish phrase druí, that means "okaytrees," and the Proto-Celtic phrase wid, meaning "to look or understand," Druidism emerges as a course rooted in know-how and a deep reference to the herbal worldwide. The Druids, because the practitioners of this historical way of life had been referred to as, were now not pleasant spiritual leaders however additionally philosophers, healers, and keepers of information. They were the realistic ones, the seers who walked a few of the geographical regions of the visible and the unseen. Their teachings had been exceeded down thru generations, frequently via oral manner of lifestyles, making them shrouded in mystique and enigma. While the Druids were commonly associated with the Celtic peoples, their have an impact on prolonged past geographical obstacles. They were acknowledged to have interacted with specific historical civilizations along with the Greeks and the Romans, leaving traces of their recognition and practices in numerous historical debts. One of the most considerable assets of information about Druidism comes from the writings of the Roman historian, Julius Caesar. In his paintings, "The Gallic Wars," Caesar gives valuable insights into the spiritual and social characteristic of the Druids inside Celtic society. He portrays them as powerful figures who held sway over the people, arbitrated disputes, and executed sacred rituals. Yet, no matter this glimpse into the arena of Druidism, loads in their teachings and practices stay veiled in secrecy. This is in detail due to the fact that the Druids did not commit their interest to writing, as they believed that data want to be surpassed on through private revel in and oral transmission. The decline of Druidism got here with the upward thrust of Christianity and the following Roman conquest of the Celtic lands. With the unfold of Christianity, the ancient traditions and ideals had been frequently suppressed, and the Druids had been relegated to the margins of society. However, the spirit of Druidism persevered, and its legacy endured to weave its manner through the cultural cloth of the British Isles. In more recent times, there has been a revival of hobby in this historical exercise, with people looking for to reconnect with the statistics of the Druids and the profound teachings they espoused. Today, Druidism stands as a testament to the long-lasting electricity of human spirituality and our innate connection to the herbal global. Its records serves as a reminder of the statistics that lies inside the depths of our ancestral information, organized to be rediscovered and embraced. In the pages that have a study, we shall adventure similarly into the coronary heart of Druidism, exploring its middle thoughts, rituals, and the profound insights it offers for our present day lives. Prepare yourself for a voyage of information and discovery as we embark in this exploration of the enigmatic and awe-inspiring worldwide of Druidism.

The Philosophy of Druidism

As we delve into the hard worldwide of Druidism, it's miles vital to apprehend the profound philosophy that underpins this ancient exercise. The philosophy of Druidism includes a deep reverence for nature, a connection to the spiritual nation-states, and a dedication to dwelling in concord with the cycles of life. At its middle, the philosophy of Druidism emphasizes the interconnectedness of all residing beings. Druids take delivery of as real with that each residing creature, from the smallest insect to the tallest tree, possesses a divine spark, a completely unique essence that contributes to the complex tapestry of existence. This perception fosters a deep understand and reverence for the herbal global, as Druids recognize that they are an essential part of a sizable and interconnected internet of lifestyles. Central to Druidic philosophy is the recognition of the inherent know-how and intelligence present in the natural international. Druids apprehend that nature isn't always in reality a backdrop for human life but a trainer and guide. By searching at and immersing themselves inside the herbal international, Druids are searching out to advantage insight and consciousness, studying from the cycles of beginning, increase, decay, and transformation which may be woven into the fabric of life itself. The philosophy of Druidism moreover emphasizes the significance of spiritual connection. Druids trust inside the life of unseen realms and spiritual beings, and they actively are seeking out to cultivate relationships with those entities. By undertaking rituals, ceremonies, and meditative practices, Druids motive to installation a deep reference to the divine, drawing thought and steerage from the spiritual geographical areas. Furthermore, Druidic philosophy encourages residing in concord with the cycles of life. Druids recognize that lifestyles is a ordinary ebb and go together with the flow, a dance between slight and darkness, increase and decay, introduction and destruction. By embracing those natural cycles, Druids are in search of to align themselves with the rhythms of the Earth and the cosmos, locating a sense of stability and harmony inside the ever-changing tapestry of life. The philosophy of Druidism additionally consists of a deep apprehend for individual freedom and personal responsibility. Druids trust inside the inherent nicely worth and sovereignty of everybody, spotting that everybody possesses the capability to make alternatives and form their very private destiny. However, with this freedom comes a profound enjoy of duty, as Druids understand that their movements have outcomes not most effective for themselves but for the broader international. In end, the philosophy of Druidism is a rich tapestry woven from threads of reverence for nature, religious connection, dwelling in concord with the cycles of lifestyles, and embracing personal freedom and duty. It is a philosophy that invitations us to step out of doors the confines of our human-centered mindset and encompass the knowledge and interconnectedness of all life. Through the philosophy of Druidism, we are invited to embark on a journey of self-discovery, connection, and concord with the herbal worldwide and the divine.

Chapter 14: Druid Practices

In the region of Druidism, the direction to enlightenment lies within the embody of ancient practices. These practices, deeply rooted in nature and the magical forces that permeate our existence, provide us a profound reference to the sacred. Through the lens of Druid practices, we're able to explore and domesticate a harmonious relationship with the herbal global and the divine. One of the vital practices loved by way of the usage of Druids is the paintings of ritual. Rituals serve as a gateway to the spiritual realm, permitting us to commune with the spirits of the land, the ancestors, and the gods. By sporting out ritual, we create a sacred region wherein the boundaries between the mundane and the transcendent blur, organising ourselves to the information and steerage of the divine. The turning of the seasons holds notable importance in Druid practices. These seasonal celebrations, known as Sabbats, mark the cycles of nature and honor the unique strength present sooner or later of every phase. From the solstices and equinoxes to the pass-vicinity days, Druids accumulate to honor the changing seasons, offering gratitude for the blessings bestowed upon us and seeking out concord with the natural rhythms of the Earth. Divination, some other vital workout in Druidism, permits us to glimpse into the hidden geographical regions and gain belief into the mysteries of lifestyles. From reading the varieties of the stars to interpreting the language of the bushes and stones, Druids are attempting to find for guidance from the forces beyond the mundane worldwide. Through divination, we tap into the collective know-how of the universe, unraveling the threads of destiny and aligning ourselves with our proper purpose. The artwork of herbalism, deeply interwoven with Druid practices, connects us in detail with the recovery energies of nature. Through the check and use of herbs, we discover ways to harness the energy of plant life to repair balance and sell well-being. Whether via crafting potions, growing sacred incense, or concocting recuperation salves, herbalism gives us a tangible manner to engage with the restoration forces of the Earth. In addition to the ones practices, meditation and contemplation form the backbone of Druid spirituality. By stilling our minds and attuning ourselves to the present 2nd, we open ourselves to the whispers of the divine. Through meditation, we cultivate inner peace, readability, and a deep revel in of reference to the herbal global. It is in the ones quiet moments of mirrored photograph that we're able to in fact pay interest the information of the bushes, the songs of the birds, and the murmurs of the ancient stones. Druid practices aren't constrained to the ones few examples; they're as numerous because the folks who examine this path. Each practitioner weaves their non-public specific tapestry of practices, drawing idea from the historic awareness and forging their private sacred connections. The splendor of Druidism lies in its adaptability and its capacity to honor the individual's adventure on the same time as embracing the collective information of the some time. In stop, Druid practices offer a tapestry of rituals, celebrations, divination, herbalism, and meditation that allow us to deepen our reference to the divine and the natural global. Through the exploration and cultivation of these practices, we embark on a profound non secular adventure, one that leads us to a more know-how of ourselves, the universe, and the interconnectedness of all topics. May those practices guide you in your private course of Druidism, illuminating your way and bringing you in the direction of the mysteries that lie within.

The Role of Nature and the Universe

The interconnectedness of nature and the universe is a important element of Druidism. In order to in reality apprehend the characteristic they play in our lives, we ought to delve deep into the essence of our existence. Nature, with its big array of vegetation and fauna, serves as a steady reminder of the splendor and power that surrounds us. It is thru nature that we are capable of witness the cyclical forms of life and death, increase and decay. The changing seasons, the ebb and flow of the tides, the growing and placing of the solar – these sorts of herbal phenomena reflect the interconnectedness of everything in the universe. As Druids, we apprehend that we aren't end up impartial from nature, but instead an essential part of it. We recognize that we are not the masters of the herbal international, however alternatively its custodians. Just as every plant and animal has its feature to play within the surroundings, so can we have our thing to meet within the grand tapestry of lifestyles. The universe, but, expands our information past the limits of our earthly life. It encompasses the vastness of region and time, and reminds us of our small vicinity indoors it. The stars, planets, and galaxies that populate the cosmos are a consistent deliver of surprise and concept. Druidism teaches us to look to the heavens with reverence and awe, spotting that the universe is a mirror of our personal internal selves. As above, so beneath – this historical maxim reminds us that the equal styles and ideas that govern the celestial our our bodies additionally govern our personal lives. By aligning ourselves with the rhythms of the universe, we can locate concord and balance inner ourselves and the arena spherical us. Nature and the universe, even though first rate in their manifestations, are intertwined in a dance of cosmic proportions. They are facets of the equal coin, reflecting the interconnectedness and interdependence that permeate all of existence. It is thru our deep connection to nature and our knowledge of the universe that we're capable of find meaning and purpose in our lives. In the exercise of Druidism, we searching out to honor and understand the herbal global, and to align ourselves with the cycles and rhythms of the universe. Through rituals, meditation, and the have a take a look at of historical understanding, we strive to deepen our know-how of the function of nature and the universe in our lives. By embracing the training of Druidism and cultivating a deep relationship with nature and the universe, we're able to tap into the profound records that lies interior us and all round us. We can discover ways to live in harmony with the herbal international and to honor the interconnectedness of all subjects. In end, the location of nature and the universe in Druidism is not certainly a philosophical concept, however a lived enjoy. It is through our deep connection to the herbal worldwide and our information of the universe that we're capable of find our vicinity inside the grand tapestry of life. May we preserve to honor and admire the splendor and strength of nature, and might we are seeking out to align ourselves with the rhythms and cycles of the universe.

Chapter 15: The Four Druidic Paths

Within the historic and mystical realm of Druidism, there exist 4 awesome paths that manual seekers on their non secular adventure. These paths, every specific in its method, offer a profound expertise of the herbal worldwide and its interconnectedness with the religious realm. In this economic damage, we are able to discover those 4 Druidic paths, delving into their standards, practices, and the information they create to those who walk upon them. First and vital, we encounter the Path of the Earth. This route emphasizes the deep connection amongst Druids and the Earth itself. It is a path that teaches us to honor and admire the land, to understand its sacredness, and to stay in concord with its rhythms. Through the Path of the Earth, Druids discover ways to attune themselves to the herbal cycles, to pay attention to the whispers of the wind, and to revel in the heart beat of the Earth underneath their ft. It is a path that invitations us to domesticate a profound reverence for the Earth and to come to be stewards of its well-being. The 2nd direction we stumble upon is the Path of the Sky. This path directs our interest to the celestial nation-states, guiding us to discover the mysteries of the celebs, the moon, and the solar. It is a route that invitations us to gaze upward and behold the vastness of the cosmos, to contemplate the celestial forces that form our global. Through the Path of the Sky, Druids learn how to find idea inside the constellations, to attune themselves to the ebb and drift of the lunar cycles, and to honor the electricity of the sun as a supply of existence and electricity. It is a path that connects us to the divine tapestry woven above, reminding us of our region in the grand cosmic layout. The 1/three direction we stumble upon is the Path of the Forest. This path beckons us into the historic woodlands, wherein the records of the trees resonates with our spirits. It is a course that teaches us to commune with the spirits of the forest, to investigate from their historic information, and to find solace in their tranquil presence. Through the Path of the Forest, Druids discover ways to attune themselves to the whispers of the timber, to are trying to find guidance from the spirits that live within them, and to embody the serenity and recovery that nature offers. It is a direction that invitations us to immerse ourselves in the beauty of the natural worldwide and to honor the spirits that are residing there. Lastly, we come across the Path of the Divine. This direction leads us to find out the geographical areas of the gods and goddesses, the deities that maintain sway over the forces of nature. It is a path that invitations us to honor and hook up with those divine beings, to are seeking for his or her steering and blessings. Through the Path of the Divine, Druids learn how to cultivate a sacred courting with the gods and goddesses, to recognize their specific traits and attributes, and to forge a deep reference to the divine inside themselves. It is a path that reminds us of our non-public inherent divinity and encourages us to stay in alignment with our maximum religious functionality. These four Druidic paths, the Path of the Earth, the Path of the Sky, the Path of the Forest, and the Path of the Divine, every offer a first rate angle at the sacredness of the natural worldwide and our region interior it. As we delve into the teachings and practices of these paths, we embark upon a transformative journey, one which permits us to hook up with the profound information of the Druids of vintage. Through their steerage, we're capable of discover a deeper understanding of ourselves, our connection to the Earth, and our area in the massive tapestry of lifestyles. May those paths eliminate darkness from our way and display the hidden truths that lie inside.

Rituals in Druidism

Rituals in Druidism preserve a profound importance in the spiritual exercise. They are the coronary coronary heart and soul of Druidic traditions, weaving a tapestry of connection some of the self, the natural global, and the divine. In this bankruptcy, we delve into the rich tapestry of rituals in Druidism, exploring their motive, office work, and transformative electricity. Druidism, at its middle, is an earth-primarily based completely spirituality that embraces the cycles of nature and seeks harmony with the living world. Rituals function a gateway to this harmony, permitting individuals to commune with the spirits of the land, ancestors, and gods. They offer a manner to honor and specific gratitude for the abundance and facts bestowed upon us thru manner of the herbal worldwide. One of the maximum vital rituals in Druidism is the birthday celebration of the seasonal fairs called the Wheel of the Year. These eight festivals mark the turning elements of the solar one year, together with the solstices, equinoxes, and the midpoints in amongst. Through those rituals, Druids attune themselves to the natural rhythms of the land, celebrating and aligning with the ever-changing seasons. Each competition inside the Wheel of the Year holds its very non-public unique significance and symbolism. For instance, on the opposition of Imbolc, taking region spherical the start of February, Druids honor the rebirth of the earth after the wintry weather close eye. They pay homage to the goddess Brigid, whose presence is felt in the awakening of life and the returning slight. Through rituals of purification and the lighting of sacred fires, Druids include the promise of new beginnings and kindle their very very own internal flame of idea. Another massive ritual in Druidism is the exercising of tree reverence. Trees are regarded as sacred beings, embodying information, strength, and a deep connection to the earth. By carrying out rituals of tree communion, Druids set up a profound bond with the ones residing entities. They seeking out steering, solace, and restoration from the ancient spirits that stay in the roots, branches, and leaves of those arboreal guardians. Through meditative practices, services, and the recitation of prayers, Druids honor the facts and interconnectedness that bushes embody. Divination is also a valuable component of Druidic rituals. The paintings of looking for steerage from the divine thru numerous techniques, which incorporates ogham staves, tarot playing cards, or scrying, is an crucial device for Druids to hook up with the unseen nation-states. Through those rituals, practitioners advantage perception into their path, collect messages from the spirits, and navigate the complexities of lifestyles with extra readability and reason. Furthermore, rituals in Druidism often incorporate the advent of sacred regions. These areas feature portals to the spiritual realm, providing a sanctuary for prayer, meditation, and connection. Whether it is thru the development of stone circles, the carving of sacred symbols, or the arrangement of altars adorned with large gadgets, the act of consecrating a location infuses it with a tangible revel in of the sacred. In prevent, rituals in Druidism are the threads that weave together the tapestry of this ancient spiritual practice. They provide a manner to honor the cycles of nature, commune with the divine, and deepen our connection to the residing international. Through celebrating the Wheel of the Year, engaging in tree reverence, running in the direction of divination, and developing sacred regions, Druids discover solace, information, and transformation. So, allow us to embark on this sacred journey together, exploring the beauty and electricity of rituals in Druidism.

Chapter 16: Symbols In Druidism

Symbols in Druidism are the critical element to knowledge the rich and profound spiritual subculture that is Druidism. Throughout the long time, Druids have used symbols as a manner of verbal exchange, a manner to connect with the divine, and a technique of retaining their sacred know-how. In this financial ruin, we will find out the significance of symbols in Druidism, their origins, and their role in current Druidic practices. One of the maximum prominent symbols in Druidism is the tree. Trees have prolonged been reputable with the aid of way of Druids as sacred beings, embodying the expertise and electricity of nature. The tree symbolizes the relationship a few of the earthly realm and the religious realm, serving as a conduit for non secular electricity. In the historic Celtic manner of lifestyles, each tree became associated with unique tendencies and attributes, imparting religious steering and perception. Today, Druids regardless of the reality that maintain the tree as a image of knowledge, strength, and harmony with the herbal global. Another essential photo in Druidism is the cauldron. The cauldron represents transformation, rebirth, and the cycle of existence. It is a vessel of divine concept and recognition, containing the capability for profound non secular growth. In Druidic rituals, the cauldron is often used to brew sacred concoctions, symbolizing the alchemical approach of religious transformation. It is thru the cauldron that Druids are looking for for to tap into the deep properly of ancestral expertise and hook up with the energies of the Otherworld. The circle is a effective image in Druidism, representing the interconnectedness of all subjects. Just due to the fact the sun rises and gadgets, the seasons exchange, and the moon waxes and wanes, the circle symbolizes the eternal cycle of existence, death, and rebirth. In Druidic ceremonies, the circle is frequently strong as a sacred area, a container for ritual and spiritual paintings. It serves as a reminder of our connection to the herbal international and the cyclical nature of lifestyles. The triskele, with its three interlocking spirals, is every one of a kind symbol of incredible importance in Druidism. Each spiral represents a one-of-a-kind element of life: the past, the prevailing, and the destiny. The triskele symbolizes the interconnectedness of time, the everlasting nature of the soul, and the cyclical nature of the universe. It is a reminder that each one things are interconnected, and that the whole lot we do has an effect on the arena around us. The final photograph we're able to explore on this monetary disaster is the Awen, a photograph of divine concept and innovative energy. Often depicted as three rays of mild radiating from 3 factors, the Awen represents the divine spark interior each people, the source of our creativity and non secular perception. Druids invoke the Awen to connect to their inner information, to are looking for steering from the divine, and to encourage their modern and non secular endeavors. Symbols in Druidism are not merely ornamental or superficial; they hold deep spiritual importance and serve as a way of verbal exchange with the divine. They are a language that transcends words, permitting Druids to tap into the historic statistics and connect to the energies of the herbal worldwide. By knowledge and running with those symbols, we will free up the profound teachings and transformative energy of Druidism.

The Role of Women in Druidism

In exploring the historic records of Druidism, it is paramount to famend and delve into the profound function of women inside this non secular subculture. The wealthy tapestry of Druidic data weaves a story that highlights the deep reverence and apprehend held for the woman divine. Through this financial catastrophe, we will embark on a journey to get to the lowest of the importance of ladies in Druidism, losing moderate on their roles, contributions, and the inherent balance they bring to this sacred course. In the place of Druidism, women have held positions of exquisite importance and authority, embodying the essence of the divine girl. They had been referred to as Druidesses, who possessed an innate connection with the herbal international and its cycles. These girls had been respected as healers, seers, and guardians of historical information. Their unique abilties to commune with nature and tap into the religious nation-states have been pretty valued, as they furnished steering, information, and insight to their groups. The Druidic tradition recognized the inherent electricity and records that ladies possessed, celebrating their capability to bring about lifestyles and nurture the growth of each the physical and non secular geographical regions. This acknowledgment of the sacred female become pondered in the rituals and ceremonies finished with the resource of Druidesses, in which they invoked the goddesses of nature, fertility, and knowledge. Through their rituals, women accomplished a essential role in attuning themselves and their groups to the rhythms of the herbal global, fostering concord and balance. One crucial element of a Druidess's feature have become the safety and transmission of oral traditions and historical know-how. They have been entrusted with the mission of memorizing and passing down the sacred records of their ancestors, ensuring its continuity for future generations. Through their characteristic as custodians of knowledge, ladies done a vital element in shaping the cultural and spiritual identification of Druidism. Furthermore, ladies in Druidism had been now not confined to precise roles or restrained in their pastimes. They had the liberty to have interaction in various additives of society, which includes politics, schooling, and imaginitive endeavors. Their voices have been valued, and their evaluations held weight in preference-making techniques. This reputation in their business enterprise and autonomy have grow to be a testament to the egalitarian nature of Druidic society. It is critical to recognize that the characteristic of women in Druidism extended past their man or woman contributions. They had been an vital a part of the hard web of interconnectedness that wove collectively the cloth of this historical religious course.

Women and men collaborated, recognizing the significance of stability some of the woman and masculine energies. Through this harmonious union, Druidism embraced the standards of duality, acknowledging that each components had been essential for the holistic boom and nicely-being of the community. In end, the function of girls in Druidism is truely one in every of massive significance. They were the keepers of ancient awareness, the conduits the numerous human and divine geographical regions, and the nurturers of balance and concord. Their contributions were imperative to the flourishing of Druidic society, and their voices echoed via the a long time, guiding and inspiring destiny generations. As we delve deeper into the nation-states of Druidism, we must honor and have a superb time the pivotal characteristic of ladies, for they may be the embodiment of the sacred lady and

the essence of this ancient spiritual
subculture.

www.ingramcontent.com/pod-product-compliance
Lightning Source LLC
Chambersburg PA
CBHW051107050726
47592CB00002B/707